Although Major Robert M. Hicks, chaplain and counselor, did not see active duty in the Middle East war, he did work behind the scenes in many capacities. In *Returning Home*, he incisively answers questions that servicemen bring home about God and their faith, along with a plethora of practical insights into postwar reintegration into family life and the work force, including:

★ A personal history of the Gulf War, consisting of vignettes of news reports, personal quotations, and published true stories by those affected by the war

★ A discussion of many vital issues:
  ★ Morality and immorality of combat
  ★ The role of "faith in the foxhole"
  ★ Unresolved conflicts at home
  ★ Financial and vocational issues
  ★ The role of celebration

★ Common questions about the Gulf War with answers from Major Hicks

RETURNING HOME

ROBERT M. HICKS

With Randy Petersen

Fleming H. Revell Company
Tarrytown, New York

Unless otherwise identified, Scripture is from the Holy Bible, New International Version. Copyright © 1973, 1978, 1984 International Bible Society. Used by permission of Zondervan Bible Publishers.
Scripture identified KJV is from the King James Version of the Bible.

Library of Congress Cataloging-in-Publication Data

Hicks, Robert.
    Returning home / Robert M. Hicks.
        p.   cm.
    Includes bibliographical references.
    ISBN 0-8007-5418-2
    1. Post-traumatic stress disorder.   2. Veterans—Mental health—
United States.   3. Persian Gulf War, 1991—Psychological aspects.
4. Persian Gulf War, 1991—Religious aspects.   I. Title.
RC552.P67H53   1991
616.85'212—dc20   91-255-12
                                                                       CIP

Copyright © 1991 by Robert M. Hicks
Published by the Fleming H. Revell Company
Tarrytown, New York 10591
Printed in the United States of America

I dedicate this book to the citizen-soldiers of the 14th Quartermaster Detachment of the Army Reserve 99 ARCOM unit in my home state of Pennsylvania. You took Saddam Hussein's best (luckiest) Scud missile shot, taking thirteen lives from your unit. For me, this was the toughest tragedy of the war. It was a senseless and tragic loss of life, especially when the unit members had only been in the region for six days, and in a few more days the war would be over. Your unit and grieving family members deserve our prayers and continued remembrance.

Contents

Preface

"Why me?" That was my reaction when I was asked to do this book. Despite my background and training in dealing with post-traumatic stress, I felt lacking in a key area: I wasn't there in the Gulf War with the other troops.

But then I thought through the involvement I did have with this war effort. I had conducted briefings with some of the departing troops, acquainting them with the differences of the Islamic religion. As a chaplain, I had counseled many of the families left behind. And as a reservist myself, I had gone through all the emotional ups and downs. Every phone call had the potential of being my notification of mobilization.

Actually, my unit *was* activated twice and then deactivated. I knew we were being factored in and out of the war plan. Since we fly the tank-killer A-10s, I felt sure we would go, especially once the shooting started. Many of my military friends were already gone, and my wife and I were spending more time on the phone with worried wives.

But I stayed behind. I began to appreciate how my father felt when he did not go to World War II because he was in the aviation industry. His job was to stay behind, make planes, and give support from a distance. This was my job as well.

In a way, we were all there. Just as when John F. Kennedy was shot, we all remember where we were that Wednesday night when the air war started. Our personal lives stopped in their tracks. Thanks to the amazing television coverage, we could participate in the war from a distance as never before. It seemed that every American knew *someone* over there, and so we were all there as well.

The war was a bomb dropped on our national life. For seven months it changed our lives, and now we're just trying to get back to normal. But how difficult will that be? What sorts of trauma did the troops face out there? What were the cameras *not* showing us? What hidden casualties of this war will surface as the troops and their friends and families try to resume their lives? These are the questions I have set about to answer.

In this book, I weave the many conversations I've had with returning vets together with the published stories of others affected by the war. In some cases, names have been changed to protect the privacy of the individuals involved. Yet the stories are true.

Finally, I must express thanks to my most able cowriter. Randy Petersen deserves much more than the byline. I dictated and wrote certain sections, but Randy took everything, made sense of it, and gave it a flow that reflected our common mind. Often his words about my words made more sense than my own. Thanks, Randy, for a job well done.

Introduction

How Susceptible Are You to Post–Gulf War Stress?

A. Who was the person closest to you who was most involved in the Gulf War?

    1. An acquaintance

    2. A good friend

    3. A family member or extremely close friend

    4. Your spouse

    5. Yourself

Answer A _____

B. What was the level of danger that person faced?

    1. Could have been called to serve but wasn't

    2. Served in a new capacity but not in the gulf arena

    3. Went to the gulf but saw no action

    4. Was close to combat action

    5. Was in the midst of combat

Answer B _____

C. Multiply answer numbers for questions A and B.

_____ X _____ = _____

  (A)   (B)   (C)

Answer C _____

D. How much has this person talked to you about his or her experiences?

1. Not at all
2. Very little
3. Has described events occasionally but with little detail
4. Has spoken once or twice, describing events in graphic detail
5. Talks often about it

(If you were involved in the war, give yourself a 4.)

Answer D _____

E. How much do you think the war has changed this person?

1. Not at all
2. Very little
3. Some, but not substantially
4. Substantial changes
5. He or she is a very different person

Answer E _____

F. Multiply answer numbers for questions D and E.

_____ X _____ = _____

  (D)   (E)   (F)

Answer F _____

G. How many people did you know who were deployed in the Middle East?

1. None
2. One
3. Two to five
4. Six to ten
5. More than ten

Answer G _____

H. On a scale of 1 to 5, how much was your family life (or individual life) disrupted by the events of the Gulf War? (1 is not disrupted at all.)

Answer H _____

I. On a scale of 1 to 5, how worried were you on January 10 (before war broke out, but with the approaching deadline) about the outcome of the war? (1 is not worried.)

Answer I _____

J. On a scale of 1 to 5, how worried were you on January 17 (the day after war broke out) about the war's outcome? (1 is not worried.)

Answer J _____

K. From January 16 on, about how much time did you spend, on the average, watching television coverage of war events?

   1. None
   2. The evening news
   3. Two to seven hours a week
   4. Seven to fifteen hours a week
   5. I was a news junkie

(If you were stationed in the Middle East, give yourself a 4.)

Answer K _____

L. For how long a period has the Gulf War disrupted your life?

   1. Not at all
   2. Two months or less
   3. Two to six months
   4. More than six months, but we're back to normal
   5. More than six months—and counting

Answer L _____

M. How helpful have friends and family been during this time?

   1. Extremely helpful
   2. Little help needed
   3. Somewhat helpful

4. I needed help, but they didn't offer or I didn't ask
5. They made things worse
Answer M _____
N. Multiply answer number for question M by 4.

$$\frac{\rule{2cm}{0.4pt}}{(M)} \times 4 = \frac{\rule{2cm}{0.4pt}}{(N)}$$

Answer N _____
Add answers C, F, G, H, I, J, K, L, and N.
TOTAL _____

Key

76–100 Get help fast. Seriously, you have been through a great deal, and you may need help sorting it all out—especially since your family and friends haven't helped much. Call a chaplain, minister, or other counselor today.

56–75 Don't be surprised if you develop symptoms of stress reaction: fatigue, bad dreams, headaches, trouble sleeping. It goes with the territory. As much as possible, talk out your worries with friends or family or a professional counselor. Read this book carefully; it will help you deal with some important issues.

36–55 You have been affected by this war but are coming through it pretty well. Still, you may need a vacation. Don't be afraid to "turn off" war thoughts by changing the subject in a conversation or in your own thinking. This book will help you sort through some issues, but put it down every so often and go out and play.

20–35 The war did not affect you greatly. Don't feel guilty about that. Look around for hurting people you can help with postwar stress.

12–19 You can be glad you suffered a minimum of worry about this war, but maybe you need to roll up your sleeves and help some others.

Part I

The Gulf War

1

The Preparation

August 2, 1990

I am in Israel, leading a study tour. We're staying at Beersheva, at the edge of the Sinai desert. The Israeli army has a headquarters there, and we suddenly notice urgent activity. Troops are hurrying here and there. Planes are taking off. Something is going on.

We rush to our televisions and radios to find out what's happening.

Iraqi forces have invaded Kuwait.

In the bubbling caldron of the Middle East, any military action can mean trouble throughout the region. Israel has never trusted Saddam Hussein. Now that he's flexing his muscles, it could be bad news for *all* his enemies, especially Israel. The whole nation braces for his next move.

Military action of this magnitude affects people all over the globe. In all our talk of resolutions and bomb tonnage and square miles and deployments, we can forget the people in the middle of all of this—the soldiers, the bystanders, the folks back home.

From the first moment, this war was touching people's lives in major ways.

It started early that morning.

Oil driller Ed Hale is working for the Kuwait Drilling Co. at Rig No. 11, near the Iraqi border. At 3:50 A.M., Charlie Amos bursts in: "There's helicopters everywhere." The long-threatened invasion of Kuwait has begun.[1]

Journalist Caryle Murphy awakens in Kuwait City a little after 5:30 A.M. There are booms in the distance. Soon Iraqi troops are battling Kuwaiti police in front of the royal palace.[2]

Shortly before 7:00 A.M., Maureen Meiers sees her Kuwaiti husband off to work and then hears bursts, like firecrackers. The sound comes from one of the royal palaces nearby. She knows it's the Iraqis. They have been poised to invade for weeks. Her husband, accosted by Iraqi soldiers on the road, escapes and hurries home.[3]

At 8:00 A.M., Kuwait time, journalist Caryle Murphy is talking on the phone with her *Washington Post* editor, describing the invasion from her window. When they wake up, United States senators will read her account of the crisis in their morning papers.[4]

Some Kuwaitis are still unaware of the invasion. A father arrives at the Ministry of Health to get some routine certificates for his newborn daughter. "Are you crazy?" the staff person tells him. "We have been invaded!"[5]

By noon, there is widespread looting in Kuwait City. Government offices are in flames. Iraqi tanks thread their way through the streets. Helicopters and jets soar overhead. Iraqi troops dig foxholes on the shore, using beach umbrellas for shade. Expensive cars are stolen and driven north into Iraq as tanks and troop carriers head south.

In America, a writer is enjoying a working vacation in New Hampshire. He strolls inside from his lakeside perch and sees a television news bulletin about this disruption half a world away. He wonders if gas prices will go up before he drives back home.

In the following days, Iraqis begin a systematic rape of Kuwait. Citizens are tortured and executed. Some go into hiding. Westerners attempt to leave the country but are usually turned back. Shops are plundered. Soldiers raid offices and apartments, destroying equipment, defacing walls, and carting off all they can carry.

The destruction and theft will continue in the coming months. An estimated $4 billion in cash and gold is taken from Kuwait's national treasury. All the books in the libraries of Kuwait University and teaching hospital Mubarak Al-Katib are taken or ruined.

Exact numbers are hard to assess, but the number of Kuwaitis killed will be in the thousands. At least 20,000 will be taken captive and deported to Iraq as slave laborers.[6]

In Jordan, there is widespread sympathy for Iraq. "We suffered while the Kuwaitis got rich and fat," says one Jordanian. "Now it's their turn to suffer."

"The Kuwaitis are thieves," says another. "Saddam is just claiming what is rightfully his."[7]

I travel to Tel Aviv and stay with a friend, his wife, and three children. Reports on television and radio are talking about gas masks. Everyone is well aware of Saddam's chemical and biological weapons. They feel he won't hesitate to use them on

Israel at the appropriate time. The government begins plans to issue gas masks to every Israeli citizen.

August 7

The deployment begins. President Bush wins approval of the first of twelve resolutions demanding Saddam's withdrawal from Kuwait and authorizing force against him. Secretary of Defense Cheney travels to the Middle East to confer with United States allies.

This massive deployment will involve the activation of thousands of reservists and National Guard forces in the United States. Twenty-eight nations will join the alliance, amassing more than 500,000 troops in the Saudi Arabian desert.

In Camp Pendleton, California, Stephen Bentzlin volunteers for an advance unit of Operation Desert Shield. This is not surprising for this young man, who was chosen Marine of the Quarter at Pendleton earlier this year. He flies to Saudi Arabia later in the month.[8]

August 12

Laura Blumenthal, an intern at the United States embassy in Amman, Jordan, writes in her diary:

> Only one Arab among the dozens I've spoken to actually criticized Saddam. The man, a policeman, described Iraq's leader as "a not good."
>
> "Then why does everyone love him so much?" I asked.
>
> The policeman said nothing. He just stood there, watching traffic, shifting his weight back and forth—right leg, left; right leg, left. I thought he didn't understand my question. Just as I began to drift down the sidewalk, he said, "People love to be slaves."[9]

August 16

Americans and Britons in Kuwait receive an order to gather at one of two city hotels. For Kuwaitis who turn in a Westerner, there is a cash bounty. For those who hide one, there is death. Some go to the hotels and are later shipped to Iraq as "human shields." Others hide and try daring escapes. One American military adviser hides in the air-conditioning crawl space of his apartment building. He watches from above as soldiers and civilians rob his apartment.

August 27

After a week and a half in hiding, reporter Caryle Murphy escapes from Kuwait, crossing the desert in a convoy of cars.[10]

In Israel, I prepare to fly home to the United States. Airport security is always tight; now it is especially so. Officials interrogate me before I leave. They seem troubled by the fact that I stayed in an Arab-run hospice in Jerusalem. That begins a new round of questions. Finally, I am cleared for departure.

On the flight, I wonder whether my reserve unit will be activated. Will I be headed right back to the Middle East in another few weeks or days?

August 29

There is news of the crash of a military transport plane at the United States base in Ramstein, Germany. A pilot's wife in New Jersey hears the report with disbelief. Her husband flies a transport plane out of Ramstein. For hours, there is no further word on the tragedy. She feels sure her husband went down. The phone rings. It's her husband. She breaks down in tears.

September 29

The 162nd Military Police Company of the National Guard, based in Crystal Springs, Mississippi, is summoned for deployment to Fort Benning, Georgia, then to Saudi Arabia. Virtually the entire town comes to the local armory to send them off.[11]

October 13

David Groce, a radio specialist, is sent to Saudi Arabia. His wife is seven and one-half months pregnant.[12]

From his post in the desert, a Marine private writes back to a schoolchild in New York: "Nothing is really happening. We sleep from 9 P.M. til 6 A.M. then train for a few hours or do nothing. Mostly the day is spent playing cards."[13]

November 12

Xavier Quinn Groce is born. His father, David Groce, phones from the gulf a few days later: "Is the baby still moving inside you?"

"I had the baby!" his wife says. "It's a boy!"[14]

A Navy doctor and his wife, stationed in Turkey, are told that she must return to the United States within two days and that he may be moved closer to the Iraq border. She hastily makes arrangements to stay with her parents on the East Coast. Four months pregnant, she hopes her husband will be able to deliver their child.

Back home in Pennsylvania, my friends are greeting me by saying, "Are you still here?" When I pick up my uniform at the cleaners, the clerk asks, "Why aren't you out in the gulf?" How can I answer?

Part of me would love to be there. That's where the action is. As a chaplain, I could have a great ministry among those frightened troops. I'm needed out in the Arabian sands.

But I'm also needed at home. I think about how my family

would be affected by my absence. How can I leave my son, my two daughters, my wife? What important family occasions—birthdays, holidays—will I miss? It's probably best for me to stay stateside.

It's out of my hands, anyway. If I'm called up, I'll go. That's my responsibility as a reservist. If I'm not, I'll stay. Those decisions, which will drastically affect me and my family, are being made somewhere else. I wish I knew what they were thinking.

It doesn't help when people keep asking why I'm still here.

December 21

At Honeywell's headquarters in Minneapolis, eight people with friends or family members in the Middle East meet with a company counselor. Honeywell feels that these people need to know they aren't alone in coping with their fears.[15]

December 31

In Rock Falls, Illinois, Laura Weed marries Tom Root, a local policeman. His National Guard unit has been called up and will ship out soon.[16]

2

The Battle

January 12, 1991

Alex Molnar, a noted pacifist, speaks to his son on the phone. Chris, 22, is a marine corporal stationed in Saudi Arabia, preparing for war. "I don't blame you," Alex says. "I'd be worried too, pal. Don't worry, kiddo, you'll come back safe. I love you, too. Very much."[1]

January 13

Churches around the country report unusually high attendance. People are gathering to pray for peace.

A homeless woman bangs a drum in the park across from the White House. "I hear that George Bush hears the drums and is disturbed," she'll say later. "I hope he gets the message: If you are killing, you are against God." The woman's daughter is in the navy and could be sent to the gulf at any time.[2]

January 14

The deadline nears. In Rye Neck, New York, third-grader Alexis Faraci says, "Well, I don't think Saddam Hussein's troops are going to leave. I mean, we only have one more day. No, I'm not too happy about it."

Lani McCann's father is in the reserves. "It may be selfish," she says, "but I don't want Dad to go."[3]

January 15

Today is the deadline for Saddam Hussein to leave Kuwait. It's also Virginia Wilson's birthday. She is a lab technician for the army, stationed in the gulf. Her husband is somewhere else in the gulf. They haven't seen each other for two months. Their three children are with grandparents in Colorado. Back in November, parents and kids were living happily at an army base in Germany. They had one week's notice to move. Now, on the eve of war, Virginia wonders whether she'll see them all again. Happy birthday.[4]

Seven hundred citizens of Crystal Springs, Mississippi, meet for prayer in the high school auditorium this evening. At least 160 of the town's residents are in the war zone. The group salutes the flag, sings "God Bless America," and hears an excerpt from a letter written by one of their servicemen to a local sixth-grader: "I tell you this so you will always know this as you are growing up: the price of freedom and democracy is high."[5]

A carpenter from New Jersey drives four hours to visit the Vietnam Veterans Memorial in the nation's capital. He leaves a note there, wrapped in a plastic sandwich bag. "Today we are at the threshold of another terrible war," it says. "I love this country, but there has got to be a better way. We do not need another wall."

Another visitor comments about the memorial: "It's almost like we're praying to it."[6]

In Boston, fifty recruits from all over New England assemble at a hotel. They will soon be in basic training. "I'm scared to die," says one, "but you don't think about that. I think once I've had training and know what I'm facing, I'll be less afraid."[7]

The Air War

January 16

I'm driving to an evening class in Theological Ethics at Villanova University. The radio crackles with the report from Baghdad. The liberation of Kuwait has begun; Baghdad is being bombed.

I take a portable radio with me into class and tell the other students the news. We gather around to hear the reports.

The professor is late; he has been watching the news reports. He looks troubled. Handing out the course outline, he says, "As you can see, I was planning to start by discussing the ethics of war, but let's put that off for another time." Class is dismissed early so we can pay full attention to the news.

A New Jersey man gets a call from a friend, asking him to say five "Hail Marys" or "Our Fathers" for peace. He agrees. "Our Father in heaven," he prays, ". . . your kingdom come, your will be done on earth as it is in heaven. . . ." He wonders what God's will is in this situation. After only three prayers, he is interrupted by another phone call. "The war's on," the caller says. He turns on CNN.

General Schwarzkopf addresses his troops just after the air assault has begun. "I have seen in your eyes a fire of determination to get this war job done quickly. My confidence in you is total, our cause is just. Now you must be the thunder and lightning of Desert Storm."[8]

Hundreds of young pilots are flying their first missions. Colonel Alton C. Whitley of the 37th Tactical Fighter Wing tells his fliers what to expect: "It would seem a little bit like fear, perhaps a little bit like anxiety. But not to worry, because we are well equipped."[9]

It's 2:28 A.M. in Baghdad. In much of the United States, it's just about time for the evening news. The Baghdad sky lights up with antiaircraft tracers. Staccato bursts are heard. Allied planes are up there somewhere in the darkness, zooming in, dropping bombs, zooming out. In Baghdad's Al Rashid Hotel, foreign journalists head for the bomb shelter. Among them is Bernard Shaw, whose CNN colleagues are still reporting from the ninth floor. "This is not what anyone expected," he says. "This is really bad."[10]

Back in Saudi Arabia, one pilot exults in a mission completed. "Coming off the target and knowing you're safe is one of the most exhilarating feelings I ever felt," he says. "It's such a feeling of relief."[11]

On the ninth floor of the Al Rashid Hotel, Peter Arnett and John Holliman continue to report the sights and sounds of the bombing to the watching world. The terrified Holliman even sticks a microphone out the window to catch the *rat-tat-tat* of the antiaircraft fire. They seem stunned by the ferocity of the attack and the futility of Iraq's defense, and they speculate about the targets—Iraqi control centers, telecommunications, ministry of defense, and so forth. In the morning, the precision of the Allied raid will become apparent.

*   *   *

In the map case inside the cockpit of an F-117A Stealth fighter is "Jeronamo," a teddy bear sent by an American woman to "Any Service Member, Saudi Arabia." SSgt. Brad Bowers comments: "I thought I'd fly it around, then send it back to her when it's all over [and] let her know where it's been." The tiny bear flies with Bowers on the Allies' first mission.[12]

The attack is "the scariest thing I've ever done," a British Tornado pilot says later. "It was absolutely terrifying. You're frightened of failure, you're frightened of dying. You're flying as low as you dare but high enough to get the weapons off. We saw some tracers coming off the target down our left side. We tried to avoid that. As the bombs come off, you just run—run like hell."[13]

The *New York Times* reports that Grand Central Station is unusually silent.[14]

In a Philadelphia suburb, one man realizes his car's gas tank is nearly empty. What will the war do to gas prices? Shrewdly (he thinks), he tears himself away from the television to drive down to the Mobil station for a fill-up. It's 9:00 P.M. and the streets are eerily quiet.

The man stops to pick up some food at Acme. The president's address to the nation is playing on the store's sound system. Saddam had his chance, the chief executive intones, but now we must force him out. The shoppers and clerks observe a glum, worried silence, punctuated only by the *beep-beep* of the product scanners.

"I support what Bush is doing," says a Los Angeles restaurant manager. "But there's definitely dissonance inside of me. The taking of lives, any lives, is hard to deal with."

A group of protesters growing to 2,500 gathers in Times Square in the hours after the attack began. "No blood for oil!" they cry. "Finally!" sighs a Seattle vendor. "Finally."[15]

The battleship *Wisconsin* sends dozens of Tomahawk cruise missiles zeroing in on key Iraqi installations. One seaman explains his feelings about firing the powerful missiles: "It's not something you can like, but you cannot dislike it so much that you can't do your job."

The firing sounds "like a giant metal door slamming," according to one reporter. The jolt rocks the ship. One specialist was choking back tears before the firing commenced. "We're tired of being here," he says. "We want to get back to our families."[16]

In Norfolk, Virginia, a group of pilots' wives gathers in the home of the squadron commander. Four televisions are tuned to different stations, a VCR hooked to each. Their husbands are in the air over Iraq. "The important thing is to be together," says the commander's wife, "not all alone, unless being alone is what you really want. What we've got is each other until we get our husbands back."

The next morning, one of the women sees her husband being interviewed. He says he feels like an athlete who went out to play the big game—only the other team didn't show up.[17]

In Rock Falls, Illinois, the town worries about the 181 members of its National Guard unit. "So many people used the Guard to supplement their income but never expected to be called," says one resident. "These are people in their thirties and forties. Their lives were mapped out. They never expected to be fighting for their country." Newlywed Laura Weed has finally put together her wedding album. "I just married him three weeks ago," she says of her Guardsman groom. "I want twenty more years."[18]

*   *   *

In a New York classroom, a fifth-grade girl worries that Iraq might bomb the United States. A boy tries to console her: "First of all, Sarah, Hussein doesn't have the bombs to reach us. Even if he did, they don't have good aim."[19]

January 17

Protesters in San Francisco disrupt the city, stopping traffic in many areas. Police arrest nearly one thousand.

An F-15 warplane is lost in combat. The colonel notes, "As the formation regrouped after hitting a target and they checked in to make a roll call, he wasn't heard from. . . . We all feel bad that we have an airplane missing, but at the same time, no one has lost his focus that we still have a job to do. I see fire in their eyes."[20]

This evening, a Scud missile is fired into Tel Aviv. Israel threatens retaliation. The world waits for Armageddon to develop. Israeli involvement will mean the pullout of Arab allies. The resulting realignment might bring about a holy war—Islam against the world. Can Israel learn *not* to retaliate?

There are several miracles here: Remarkably few in Israel will be killed in the Scud attacks, and Israel exercises amazing restraint. Armageddon is averted, for now.

January 19

A woman writes from the Tel Aviv area:

> These past few days, and especially the nights, have been very tense. When the sirens go off—we've had real alarms at 2 A.M. and 7 A.M.—we jump up to gather the girls into our bedroom, which has been sealed hermetically against a possible gas attack. After getting our own gas masks on and

helping the girls with theirs, we seal the door to the room with packaging tape and lay a towel soaked in a weak bleach solution at its base to prevent gas from seeping in. Then we put on long clothing in case damage to the building forces us to evacuate during a gas attack. We thank God that to date no chemical weapons have been used . . . we are drained from all this "excitement." Our sleep patterns are off and civil defense orders have kept us all basically "restricted to barracks" since Tuesday night. We all need to get outside and breathe some fresh air, but it's hard to know when we'll be able to safely do that.[21]

January 20

Saddam Hussein announces on Iraqi radio, "The infidel tyrant's missiles and aircraft are being destroyed. His defeat will be certain."[22]

Major Jeffrey Tice and Captain Harry Roberts are reported missing in action as their planes fail to return to base. Later Iraqi television broadcasts videos of the two, in addition to other captured fliers. The scarred face of another downed flier, Lieutenant Jeffrey Zaun, makes the cover of *Newsweek,* shocking Americans into the awareness of the human cost of war.

In South Carolina, a support group for pilots' wives is doing extra business these days. Wives are worrying to a greater degree after seeing the videos of the POWs. That, combined with the fatigue of one week of war action, has them fighting depression. "I had a real sinking feeling [after watching the tapes], like a terrible realization that the war most definitely had hit home," says one navy wife. Another explains that she and others are trying to get their lives back to normal as much as possible—and to watch less television. "For the first few days," she says, "all of us wives were glued to the television, holding on to each other for mutual support. But life goes on. We're going to see this

through in good shape and keep things going back here on the
home front. We're fine.''[23]

Out in the desert of southern Iraq, Major Jeffrey Tice is captured by Bedouin nomads. They argue over whether to shoot him
or slit his throat. Then the Bedouin chief comes upon Tice's
family pictures in his wallet—his wife and two children. He
looks closely at each photo, then kisses each one and puts them
in Tice's lap. Then he orders that Tice be untied and seated at his
right side, a place of honor.[24]

A C-5 supply plane flies into Dhahran, Saudi Arabia, and
prepares to fly out again. But the crew is asked to take 73 civilian
passengers with them. Sixty of these are children. Crew members
carry the kids up the steep steps, but before they can fully board,
there is a Scud alert. Two Patriot missiles engage the incoming
missile with a huge bang, and all in the area retreat to their
shelters. There is always the danger of poisonous gas.

The C-5 crew hands the children down the steps, and all hurry
to the shelter. The children have no gas masks. Soon the all clear
sounds and they board the plane again. When all but one or two
are on the plane, there's another air-raid siren. Another evacua-
tion. Another all clear. But before they can reboard, there's a
third siren.

"Is this an actual attack?" the C-5's colonel, Paul Weaver,
asks the tower. The answer comes through a gas mask: Yes, it is.

As the passengers gather again in the unsealed shelter, Weaver
is told that this is "condition black"—there *are* chemical agents
in the air. He and two colleagues look around at the children,
who will die there without masks. One by one, they take off their
own masks. They will not stand and watch the children die.

Twenty minutes later it is announced that a mistake was made.
One airman had had an epileptic seizure, similar to the effects of

chemical weapons. All is clear. Quickly and happily, the passengers board the C-5 and fly to safety.[25]

By now, Baghdad is crippled: no electricity, no running water, no telephones. Streets are empty, shops closed.[26]

Four-year-old Joey is living with his grandparents in Ohio because both Mom and Dad are stationed in the gulf. Seeing an explosion on television, he asks, "Did my mommy and daddy just get killed?"
"No," says Grandpa.[27]

The barrage on Baghdad continues, with astonishing precision. Tomahawk cruise missiles are regularly seen sailing through the streets of the city, between buildings, around cars. A reporter for the Reuters news service actually sees a missile arrive at a street corner, seem to stop for a moment, and turn left.[28]

In Ohio, a colonel explains to families of the local reserve group that they should only come to the army reserve center once a week. With the reserve unit stationed in the gulf, some family members have been coming to the center round-the-clock to watch the news and support one another. But the colonel is worried about terrorism; the center is a potential target. Still, one relative asks, "What happens at 1:00 A.M. when I'm about to crack?"[29]

Israeli writer David Grossman tells of his sons, five and eight years old, who decided to run away from home. "They were ringing the doorbell a few minutes later, asking for their gas masks."[30]

January 24

A Christian radio program based near Chicago institutes a Desert Storm hotline. Callers can hear a three-minute message on

some spiritual issue pertaining to the gulf conflict. Radio stations
are even invited to record the daily message and play it on the air.
Listeners can also receive a Desert Storm Prayer Guide to help
them pray. Suggestion 1: "Pray that the power of evil will be
contained—in individuals, in military commanders, and in leaders of nations, including those of the allied coalition as well as
those in Iraq."[31]

Marine Stephen Bentzlin, near the Iraqi border, calls his wife,
Carol. In the two-hour call, they discuss finances, even possible
funeral arrangements in case he doesn't return. Later he calls his
father in Minnesota, waking him up at 4:00 A.M. and engaging in
small talk.[32]

January 29

Iraqi forces attack the Saudi town of Khafji, and the world
wonders why. Allied troops are surprised but eventually fight to
reclaim the village. A number of Allied soldiers are killed, seven
by a United States missile.

January 30

A chaplain comes to the door of a house in Camp Pendleton,
California, in his crisp blue uniform. Marines stand on either
side. Carol Bentzlin opens the door and receives word that her
husband, Stephen, died at Khafji. "I'm trying hard not to think
of him," she tells a reporter later. "Logically, I know he's
gone."

In Wood Lake, Minnesota, Stephen's hometown, people try to
support his mother in the following days. "This whole town
hurts," says the Methodist pastor.[33]

January 31

Melissa Rathbun-Neely, a twenty-year-old army driver, becomes the first woman declared missing in action. She and part-

ner David Lockett were driving a heavy truck near the Kuwaiti border and got stuck in the sand. The Iraqis boast that they have female POWs. Family and friends back in Newaygo, Michigan, worry about Melissa, though everyone says she's tough as nails. Torture? Rape? Who knows what the Iraqis might do?

"I'd like to think she wouldn't talk back to her captors," says Melissa's first-grade teacher, "but I wouldn't bet on it. She had a lot of spice to her."[34]

3

The Victory

February 5, 1991

A man writes from Tel Aviv:

> Life has slowly begun to return to normal here with people
> back at work and children returning to school. The reason is
> not a lessening of the danger (in fact, as Saddam is pressed
> to the wall it is even more likely that he will try to use
> chemical weapons against us) but economic necessity: the
> factories must operate to keep the national economy alive
> and working mothers must have a place for their children to
> be supervised. Perhaps a symbol of the Israeli determination
> to live "normally" in this abnormal situation is the appear-
> ance of designer gas mask totes on the market.
>
> Several [of our friends] have had their windows shaken
> by nearby hits. One . . . was temporarily evacuated from
> her building when a missile landed nearby but did not det-
> onate. Apparently an angel caught the thing and laid it down
> nice and gently.[1]

February 9

Thom Jenkins returns home to Coulterville, California, in a casket covered with a flag. The twenty-one-year-old was killed, perhaps by friendly fire, in a skirmish near the Kuwait border. "People do view him as a hero," says his father. "To me, he's my son. . . . Please be kind. Please be honest. Don't be too big, because it's not real."[2]

February 16

General Norman Schwarzkopf says in an interview:

> I don't want to kill one more American! I don't want to see one more American die—be it from an accident or from battle. There's no bloodlust on the part of myself or anybody else around here. What we want to do is to accomplish the objectives of this whole thing, get it over with as quickly as we can, and get back home. And I tell you, that's the attitude of everybody from the top general down to the lowest private.[3]

General Colin Powell and Secretary of State Dick Cheney visit a Stealth fighter squadron in the desert. As is the custom, they join the troops in writing messages on the bombs. Powell scrawls a note to Saddam on a laser-guided bomb: "You didn't move it, so now you lose it."[4]

Saddam Hussein, says one American paratrooper, "hasn't done anything but strike out. Now he is standing at the plate without a bat and doesn't know it."[5]

Ground soldiers worry about encountering chemical weapons in combat. "You cannot see it, you cannot feel it, it is going to kill you," says one tank sergeant near the border. "That is the evil mystique."[6]

Radios in the gulf can pick up propaganda from Iraq, including the voice of a woman the soldiers have dubbed Baghdad Betty. "Your wives back home are being unfaithful to you," she teases, claiming that they are having affairs with various television celebrities (including Bart Simpson!).[7]

Correspondent Ray Wilkinson writes from Saudi Arabia:

> The mail truck arrives at dusk each evening from the rear and looks of pure dejection flash across the faces of those who don't get letters. Those who do walk off alone into the desert. Many then tear up their letters and bury the pieces in the sand. The troops are instructed not to carry anything with names and addresses or personal information. They might, after all, be taken captive, and should bear nothing that would give enemy interrogators a psychological edge. Some Marines say they have sent photographs of their loved ones home. Others insist they will carry their most valuable mementos—without names or addresses—with them into battle.[8]

A nineteen-year-old writes to his mother in Atlanta. "If I kill anyone over here, will that change anything between us?"
She writes back: "Nothing you ever do will make me not love you. I am your mother."[9]

A test pilot writes to his wife in Tennessee: "I won't lie, it's scary. Your stomach muscles tighten . . . I think of how nice it would be to be home again. I don't like killing people and may God forgive me."[10]

An army specialist writes to his wife in El Paso:

I've taken advantage of the endless hours of waiting. I've been going to a Bible study a couple of nights a week. It's really enlightening. I can fully understand now why God placed key figures of biblical times into the desert for days, months, even years at a time. In some ways, it's very cleansing. . . . The difficulty for me at this point is simply homesickness.[11]

"There are favorite songs, including one that is making the rounds of tents and bunkers in northern Saudi Arabia. It is a verse for the soldier, the 91st Psalm.

"Under his wings you will find refuge. His faithfulness is a shield and buckler."[12]

The Ground War

February 23

In the gulf, Pfc. Tony Morales tells of a dream he had last night. "I am the first into the trenches. I throw a grenade, but it doesn't explode. I zero in on an Iraqi. He is also aiming at me, but I pull the trigger first." He seems worried about the impending conflict but then shrugs, "If old J.C. up in the sky pulls my card, there's nothing I can do about it, is there?"[13]

In international capitals, peace talks have been swirling. President Bush has set a firm deadline: get out by noon Saturday, or we'll chase you out. The deadline passes.

President Bush makes a statement Saturday night: "I have therefore directed General Norman Schwarzkopf, in conjunction with coalition forces, to use all forces available, including ground forces, to eject the Iraqi Army from Kuwait."[14]

The attack begins at 8:00 P.M. United States Eastern time, 4:00 A.M. in the desert. It is a "fake right, left hook" combination that works to perfection. A huge amphibious force sits in the gulf as a decoy. Iraqi forces expect an attack on Kuwait from the sea. Instead, land forces storm into Iraq far to the west, defeating weaker forces and cutting off the Iraqis' retreat from Kuwait.

February 25

In the United States, there is concern as the offensive begins. Initial reports indicate little Iraqi resistance. Concern turns to bewilderment. The news can't possibly be this good. More reports come through, almost monotonous in their content: Iraqis are surrendering faster than the Allies can accept them. It is a rout. The bewilderment turns to the joy of victory.

A United States Humvee (a jeeplike vehicle) is stuck in the mud. (Yes, mud. Rain in the desert was making the terrain gooey.) The lone driver watches as an Iraqi tank and another armored vehicle approach. In any normal war, he's a dead duck. In this war, however, the Iraqis pull the Humvee out of the mud and surrender to the driver.[15]

February 26

The Iraqis have left Kuwait City. A Kuwaiti flag flies from the police station. The city is one big party. Crowds fill the streets. Some shoot guns into the air. Others are injured by the falling bullets.

In a show of military protocol, Arab troops are allowed to enter the city first, to "liberate" it. But later the entering American soldiers are thronged by well-wishers. "George Bush, very, very, very, very, very, very, very, very, very good," says one old man. "Welcome to your country," says a woman.[16]

One tank unit chases the fleeing Iraqi troops, but a few Iraqis put up a fight. A first lieutenant tells of passing a seemingly abandoned tank when an Iraqi jumps out and levels a rocket launcher at him. He's a goner, for sure. Then he hears a double bang. Looking up, he sees that his major has shot the Iraqi and that the tank has blown up in the process. "I killed my first man today," says the major, "and I'm not sure I feel very good about it."[17]

The rout continues. Iraqi soldiers are surrendering to anyone who will take them, even journalists.

Reporter Tony Clifton writes:

> The initial shelling had blocked the road off [on which many Iraqis were trying to escape], and a vast traffic jam of more than a mile of vehicles, perhaps 2,000 or more, had formed behind it. Allied jets had then repeatedly pounded the blocked vehicles. As we drove slowly through the wreckage, our armored personnel carrier's tracks splashed through great pools of bloody water. We passed dead soldiers lying, as if resting, without a mark on them. We found others cut up so badly, a pair of legs in its trousers would be 50 yards from the top half of the body. Four soldiers had died under a truck where they had sought protection. Others were fanned out in a circle as if a bomb had landed in the middle of their group.[18]

A cease-fire is declared for midnight, United States Eastern time, after one hundred hours of fighting. Harsh terms are imposed on the defeated Iraqis.

February 28

Ruth Dillow of Chanute, Kansas, receives word that her son, Pfc. Clayton Carpenter, has been killed. The twenty-year-old tank mechanic had been serving near the Kuwaiti front, officials said, and was hit by a cluster bomb.[19]

*   *   *

Future plans? Private Tony Morales is glad he has a future. "What I don't plan on doing is ever going to the beach again. I never, never want to see sand again in my life."[20]

March 1

Ruth Dillow of Chanute, Kansas, receives a call late at night. "Hi, Mom. This is Clayton."
"Are you sure?" she asks. "You've been declared dead."
He had been lightly wounded in the hand and foot but was still alive and kicking—well, *alive* anyway.[21]

The party goes on in Kuwait City. Four teenage girls are seeking autographs from American soldiers and reporters. They wear sweaters with portraits of George Bush, John Major, and Margaret Thatcher. One reporter, besieged for an autograph, writes: "To Maha, on a wonderful day, 3-1-91."[22]

American soldiers act like tourists, photographing one another in front of wrecked tanks or other landmarks. One member of a transportation unit has a picture taken with Iraqi POWs, then sends the photo home to his father.

A couple of army intelligence officers survey the carnage on the roads leading out of Kuwait. Iraqi vehicles and bodies are mangled together, a result of the Allies' relentless bombing. "Some of these guys weren't but 13, 14 years old," says one.[23]

A correspondent, after visiting the scene of this carnage, writes:

> I walked along for a while with . . . a major in the Army's
> special operations branch . . . who served in Vietnam and

has seen more of this sort of thing than he cares for. I liked him instantly, in part because he was searching hard to find an acceptance of what he was seeing. He said he felt very sad for the horrors around him and had to remind himself that they were once men who had done terrible things. Perhaps, he said, considering the great casualties on the Iraqi side and the extremely few Allied deaths, divine intervention had been at work—"some sort of good against evil thing." I liked him best because he settled on not a rationalization or a defense but on the awful heart of the thing, which is that this is just the way it is. "No one ever said war was pretty," he said. "Chivalry died a long time ago."[24]

March 4

Melissa Rathbun-Neely, the female POW, is released. "They were the nicest people," she says of her Iraqi captors. "They did all they could to make me comfortable. I'm probably the only POW who has ever gained weight." The Iraqis told her she was "as brave as Sylvester Stallone and as beautiful as Brooke Shields." She says she spent most of her captivity in isolation, reciting poems and singing songs from her childhood.

How is she handling hero status? "I don't know what I'm a hero about," she says. "I just got stuck in the sand."[25]

The Aftermath

A father receives a photo of his son with Iraqi POWs. He has been worried about his son for months but consoled himself with the thought that the son was merely in a transportation unit, close to combat action but not in it. But, seeing this picture, the closeness of it all, the imminence of the danger that has just passed, gets through to him. The father begins to have bad dreams.

A twenty-three-year-old infantryman returns home and can no longer get along with his wife. They file for divorce. "I was fighting for a way of life,'' he says, ''but when I came back my way of life was gone.''[26]

Postwar reports indicate that, of 450 women on the USS *Acadia* during the conflict, 36 were pregnant. Fourteen of these were already pregnant when their seven-month assignment in the gulf began. But the other 22 apparently became pregnant during the conflict. Yet the navy assures us that it knows of no improper fraternization among crew members. It *is* possible that the women became pregnant on shore leave. Still, some are calling the *Acadia* ''The Love Boat.''[27]

A returning sergeant finds his infant child now walking and talking. ''I've missed seven months of the most important part of their lives,'' he complains.[28]

Another sergeant meets his seven-month-old daughter—born two days after he left for the gulf. ''Does she always whine like this?'' he asks his wife.[29]

His first night back, a marine wakes up screaming: ''Hurry up! Hurry up! We gotta dig out!''[30]

An air force major spends his first day home praying and playing with his three kids. His twenty-two-month-old daughter looks completely different from when he left. ''When I walk out the door now,'' he says later, ''my little girl says, 'Daddy leaving?' and you can almost see the tears in her eyes.''[31]

An army reserve engineer calls his company in Pennsylvania, looking to return to his job. He learns he has been laid off.[32]

Two months after the liberation of Kuwait, a unit of marine reservists is still camped out on Hill 99, somewhere west of Kuwait City. Among the first units into Kuwait, they captured

230 Iraqis, occupied this hill, and won an award as best combat reserve unit. And then, they think, they were forgotten.

"Three times they've told us we'd be home in seven to fourteen days," says a major. "They tell us this every seven to fourteen days." On his T-shirt are the words, "Kuwait, Therefore I Wait."

"We have no purpose," says a corporal. "We call ourselves the lost boys."[33]

At this writing, Saddam Hussein remains in power. He savagely put down a rebellion and mistreated the Kurds. Reports say he is rebuilding his army. Many Americans wonder whether it was all worth it. Some feel that Allied forces should have done more to remove Hussein and obliterate his power. Others are very glad the war ended when it did.

Part II

The Many Faces of
War Trauma

4

The Wounds of War

War hurts people.

That sounds simple enough, but we don't always recognize how wide-ranging the damage of war is. No matter how justified the war may be, no matter how necessary, no matter how one-sided its outcome, the violence of war bombards both victor and victim at many levels.

Parades are nice. Every day, it seems, television chronicles the return of some local hero. We wave our yellow ribbons to celebrate the fact that our veterans are coming home, safe and sound. But *how* sound? What damage was done to those apparently healthy returnees of this conflict? What innocence was lost in those Arabian sands? How have these soldiers changed, and how have their families changed as they watched and waited?

Granted, the Gulf War was relatively painless for the Allies. There were minimal casualties. Considering the huge array of troops deployed, this was miraculous. But any war takes its toll on the minds and hearts of its participants, and we must take this into account. We must be ready to treat the hidden emotional wounds that will become apparent over the next few years.

In the first three chapters, we have seen what war costs, not in terms of budgets and defense outlays but in terms of *people*.

There are those like Carol Bentzlin and the Jenkinses, mourning the loss of husbands and sons. There are those who wake up at night with memories of the men they shot. There are parents who have missed crucial times in their children's lives. And always, there are the children themselves, worrying and wondering.

Yes, there were some magnificent moments in those months of conflict: pilots nobly giving up their gas masks; the growth that occurs in quiet times in the desert; the many letters and teddy bears and yellow ribbons that offered support from the folks back home; the celebration of a liberated Kuwait.

I don't for a moment want to deny that American forces performed admirably under some difficult circumstances, but we can't just turn the page and move on to new national crazes. We must care for the many who need helping. We must understand their needs.

Where do you hurt right now? As a returning vet, as a faithful family member, as a supportive citizen, what toll has the war taken in your life? Don't let the world rush you forward before you stop and get the healing you need.

Response to Trauma

To some extent, everyone involved in the Gulf conflict, including the families of service personnel, suffered a trauma. At minimum, everyone in the gulf experienced upheaval and imminent danger. Those in the heat of the conflict faced difficult experiences, and some saw the death or serious injury of close friends. Whatever the circumstance, *trauma* was involved, and it would help to have some understanding of what trauma is and how it affects a person.

Trauma is the Greek word for "wound." We use the term to denote the lasting effects of a catastrophe. A traumatic experience is a catastrophe that leaves a painful impression. When a soldier is struck by a bullet, the physical catastrophe of being shot is a single event, over in a second, but the trauma has just begun. The same is true when a soldier sees his buddy struck by a bullet. This is an emotional catastrophe, followed by emotional trauma. As the Greek word indicates, when a person encounters a trauma, he is wounded. With all wounds, there must be a time of healing, and often there are scars that will last forever.

People react to trauma in many ways, ranging from emotional to purely physical. Possible symptoms include:

• **Emotional symptoms:**   Fear, anxiety, inability to concentrate, withdrawal, guilt, and shame.

• **Psychophysical symptoms:** Hyperalertness, exaggerated startle response, tremors, memory impairment, sleep disturbance, crying, flashbacks, "hysterical" paralysis or blindness.

• **Physical symptoms:**   Exhaustion, hyperventilation, heart palpitations, increased pulse or blood pressure, anorexia, nausea, cramps, urinary frequency, muscular tension.

This is, of course, a grab bag of symptoms. Ten individuals experiencing the same trauma may exhibit ten different symptoms at ten different times. Yet the range of symptoms shows us how deeply trauma affects us. Even when we think we've handled a traumatic event pretty well, some traumatic responses may still appear. This does not necessarily mean we're sick; it means we've been wounded.

We might liken trauma to the effect of a wrecking ball on a ten-story building. The ball pounds into the first floor, breaking and bending the supporting beams, smashing all it touches. The structure suffers trauma; it has been wounded. Then parts of the upper floors collapse because they have nothing to hold them up, even though the wrecking ball never touched them.

Similarly, each of us has certain emotional structures we have built up over time. We base our lives on assumptions such as:

"Nothing really bad will happen to me."

"The things that happen in life make sense."

"Good things happen to good people."

"I am basically in control of my life."

"I am basically a good person."

Some of these concepts are built into our religions. Now some Christians would say, "No, I am not in control of my life; God is." And yet, when pressed, they'd have to admit that they think God pretty much lets them run their own show.

These are our "first floor" assumptions. But when a spouse, a child, or a fellow soldier dies suddenly, when events spin out of our control, when a senseless catastrophe occurs, the wrecking ball plunges into our first floor of assumptions and throws our whole emotional structure into trauma. We begin to doubt everything, fear everything, rage at everything.

The repair of our "ten-story building" depends on how strong the structure is, how hard the wrecking ball hit, and what sort of workers and equipment are available to shore it up. You've probably picked up the analogy: "Stronger" people tend to weather tragedies better; more serious tragedies create more lasting problems; and people with devoted, wise, and immediate support tend to come out of trauma in pretty decent shape.

But if those support workers don't move in right away to shore up the failing structure, the rest of the building begins to fall apart. Jobs may be lost; marriages may crumble; self-respect may dissolve.

This book is an effort to help you understand trauma recovery, to show you—families and friends of those returning from the

Gulf conflict and you returning vets yourselves—how to make things better.

It's Normal

The most important thing to remember about post-traumatic response is this: *It is normal.* It is normal to respond in abnormal ways to abnormal circumstances.

As returning soldiers deal with flashbacks of their violent encounters, their first fear is usually, "I'm going crazy!" The fact is, such reactions are normal. These people have been thrown into abnormal situations. Things happened to shake their most basic assumptions; the wrecking ball comes crashing into their lives. *Of course* they will react. It would be stranger if they didn't.

This is true at every level of trauma. Those who never saw combat may still have trouble readjusting to life at home. They may experience unprovoked anxiety attacks as a delayed reaction to the uncertainty of Desert Shield's waiting days. This, too, is normal.

Husbands and wives who were apart for six or nine months may very well find it difficult to live together again. They may fear that their marriage is on the rocks, but this is not necessarily true. They are merely going through a time of adjustment, a reaction to the abnormal conditions of wartime.

So don't panic. You will have to make some adjustments. It may take some time to heal. Patience is hard to find in this world of "now!" But stay with it, stay open, seek help wherever you can find it.

5

Like Nothing We've Ever Seen

Welcome to war in the twenty-first century. All right, I may be jumping the gun, so to speak, but the Gulf War was a new kind of conflict. Total force. Technobattle. Precision bombing. CNN. We've never seen anything quite like it.

They say that every general wants to refight his last war. In a way, that's what Saddam was doing. Iraq had just been enmired in a long, costly ground war with Iran. It was trench warfare, a throwback to World War I, and Iraq gave every impression of following the same game plan for this war. Trenches were dug; barriers were erected; mines were laid. Even the threat of chemical weapons smelled vaguely like the poison gas of World War I.

But General Schwarzkopf and the Allied forces were not fighting the *last* war but the *next* one: Stealth bombers; laser-guided missiles; missiles that follow directions to a target better than a cab driver ever could. This was World War I against World War III. You can't fight progress.

The differences of this war make its aftermath uncertain. How should we recover from the conflict? We don't know. We've never been through this before; new rules apply.

Consider Vietnam. *That* was a different war. We had to learn how to fight it as we went along. We also had to learn how to recover from it, something we didn't do very well.

A nation of winners, we found it hard to look Vietnam's "losing" veterans in the eye. (Of course, it was not "they" who lost it but all of us. Still, we were embarrassed. We didn't know how to lose.) As a result, many of these vets *still* haven't recovered, two decades later.

New wars demand new ways. We will discover new needs in the aftermath of the Gulf conflict. We must be alert to these needs and sensitive to their distinctiveness.

Huge deployment Seldom have so many been mobilized so quickly. Vietnam's escalation was long and drawn out. We have to go back to World War II to find such a massive activation of American troops.

This means that many, many families were affected. The war was a national effort. We all felt very much involved. We all went through the roller coaster of emotions—anxiety, worry, sorrow, joy. Many put in extra effort to compensate for the absence of a person serving in the gulf, or to help a family. Many grandparents and aunts and uncles were pressed into service as long-term baby-sitters. Many spouses became single parents for an extended time and had to lean on friends and neighbors for support.

In short, we're all stressed out. We all feel that we've been through a lot—and we have, some more than others. We all feel that we need a vacation. *We've* been giving and giving and giving, and now we feel someone else should give to us. But who? Everyone feels the same way.

Imagine the wife who has been serving in Dhahran while her husband stayed home with the kids. She is tired of sand and

Scuds and silly restrictions. He's tired of the whole Mr. Mom routine. She arrives home saying, "At last I can relax!" He greets her thinking, *Great! Now she can do the housework!* There will be an explosion in that home unless they talk through their conflicting expectations.

In a way, our whole nation is like this. We expect everyone else to help us deal with our stress, but they're all busy dealing with their own.

At a national level, we have to allow a readjustment period. We can't expect things to get back to normal right away; there are just too many people involved.

Limited action, few casualties   Many of those deployed in the gulf arena just sat there. They were backups, support personnel, or decoys. This is not to say that they weren't important. Their presence was crucial to the proper operation of the Allied strategy, but they still didn't have much to write home about.

If the war had lasted longer, it would have been different. If the ground war had gone as expected, dragging on for weeks and months, these forces would have been pressed into action. But thankfully, this wasn't necessary.

This presents us with two unique sets of problems. The first is the guilt of passivity. "I sat and played cards while others risked their lives." They are hailed as heroes, but they feel undeserving.

One reservist tells of being accosted in the Atlanta airport by a "little old lady." He was wearing his desert camouflage, so she recognized him as a Desert Storm vet. She approached him and said, "Can I hug you? I'm so grateful to you!" And he's thinking, *Do I know this woman? Did I help her cross a street once?*[1]

Yes, it's nice to be thanked, and this is light-years better than tales of Vietnam vets being abused in airports. But still, the hero worship can be a bit hollow for many.

Related to this feeling may be bitterness and low self-esteem.

"You send me halfway across the world and then you bore me to death. Thanks a lot." Some inactive soldiers can be like the veteran second baseman who is benched so the rookie can learn to play: "Why am I even on the team if you aren't going to use me?"

Others may secretly feel that they weren't good enough for war action. Although this is almost certainly not the case—many fine units did not see action—their inactivity can underscore feelings of inadequacy.

A second round of problems involves those who really were hurt in the gulf. A number of vets are returning with physical injuries. Not all of those Iraqi mines were swept up. Others have serious mental or emotional problems stemming from the war.

As long as we have the image of this war as "easy," as "painless," we will try to ignore those who did sustain injuries or the families who lost loved ones. They present us with a truth we'd rather not face: War hurts.

The best way to deal with these unique problems is simply to face up to the truth and talk about it. First, we can affirm the inactive Desert Storm vets for what they actually did—which is considerable. They disrupted their lives to make themselves available if necessary. They spent months in a scary situation of readiness and impending conflict. And they lived for six weeks in the shadow of Scuds. Second, we must admit that this war *was* costly to those who sacrificed their lives or their health for the nation's cause. Let's not forget these people.

Involvement of reserve forces and National Guard units.   For the last decade, the United States armed forces have pushed the "readiness" issue and the "total force" concept. Training was geared for events just like this. Previously, a reserve or National Guard unit could be seen as a club to join or a way to pick up extra bucks, but the entire idea did a turnaround in the eighties. These

were fighting forces. Training had to be first-class; equipment
had to be first-class; commitment had to be first-class.

Still, such an adjustment is not made overnight. For many in
the reserves and National Guard, activation seemed a distant
possibility. Surely we had enough active-duty forces to deal with
any situation that might come up, short of World War III. Or so
they thought.

So it came as a shock to many when they were required to
leave their homes, their jobs, their community responsibilities to
serve in the gulf. In many cases, military pay was less than their
salaries at the jobs they left, adding an unexpected economic
burden.

Military "readiness" was a concern shortly before the war
began. As it turned out, it didn't seem to be a problem. But
emotional readiness may be a different story. Were the reservists
and Guardsmen and their families prepared for this kind of commitment? Not always. Maybe they should have been, but not all
of them were.

We will find some of them recovering from a type of shock.
Some marriages will fall apart; some people will fall apart. Some
will not be able to handle the stresses involved in the readjustment to normal life—catching up with the kids, paying the bills
when you've been at half-salary for six months (or just getting
your old job back). There's a whole new round of battle to do at
home, and many of these part-time soldiers just aren't ready
for it.

There will be some bitterness, not at the level of Vietnam, but
something similar to the attitude of draftees. "The military has
messed up my life, changed my plans, squashed my dreams,
destroyed my marriage, wiped out my savings." Hey, that was
part of the deal, we might say. That was a chance they took. But
bitterness goes beyond logic. The wise friend won't argue but
will start putting the pieces back together.

Consider the reservists on Hill 99 in Kuwait. They've done a great job, and they were happy to serve their country by doing it. But now they want to get back home. Instead, they've languished for two months on this hill in the middle of nowhere, awaiting orders to move. "Aren't there active-duty people who can do this?" they wonder.

The bitterness of reservists and Guardsmen may be compounded by their sense of being treated as second-class soldiers. This shouldn't happen, but don't kid yourself, it does. When you consider their first-class sacrifices, this can be especially upsetting.

War by technology   Never before have we seen such sophisticated weaponry. It boggles the mind to consider its precision. Early in the air war, television viewers saw tapes of bombs finding the tiniest of targets—the proverbial needle in a haystack. We have entered the era of "smart bombs." You don't have to drop them on the target. You don't have to aim them. Just put them up there and they'll find their own way.

Think about what this does to warfare. Well, there's good news and bad news.

The good news is that greater precision means fewer civilian deaths. In World War II the margin of error in bombing was about one mile. You could aim for a military target in a city and hit a hospital or school in the same city. (You would also drop more bombs to be sure you hit the target.) In Vietnam, it was about a quarter of a mile—better, but still far from precise. But some of the weapons used in Desert Storm have an accuracy range as low as 100 feet. So even if the bomb itself misses the target, the explosion will still hurt it. This means you can get by with fewer bombs, those bombs can get by with less explosive power, and accidental civilian deaths will be very few. You could bomb a military target and leave a hospital next door untouched (this, in fact, happened in raids on Baghdad).[2]

But the computerization of war has a downside to it, too. Now, you don't have to see your victims. Just punch in the coordinates. You can practically run a whole war by computer and never see a dead body. It's like playing a video game.

When you actually see that there are people in that square mile you're obliterating with your bombs, that can be a shock. When you enter Iraq after the war and see the dead bodies, that's when you realize the full effect of what you've done. It's not a video game anymore.

You need to do some "moral homework" to kill somebody, even for just cause. A police officer goes to work with the understanding that he or she may have to shoot somebody for certain reasons in certain circumstances. The moral justification is worked out in advance and afterward, in the substantial debriefing that follows a shooting. In conventional warfare, each soldier expects that he may have to shoot someone. That's what he's there to do. But increasingly, a computer technician, other specialist, or a pilot can forget that he is killing people—and fail to do the moral homework necessary. When it suddenly becomes real, he may be wracked with guilt and remorse. He's not ready for it.

Television coverage   We watched this war from start to finish. This was pretty amazing, considering the censorship imposed on both sides and the danger of being a Western journalist in Baghdad.

Still, we got the story from Baghdad, from Dhahran, from Riyadh, and eventually from Kuwait City. We had a front-row seat for the whole conflict.

This has several implications. First, spouses and other loved ones could be thoroughly involved in the war—perhaps too involved. In the aftermath of this war, even television watchers can suffer from a form of battle fatigue.

Second, this may create communication problems with returning soldiers. We viewers think we know this war, but we weren't really there. We never felt the sand, the fleas, the boredom. And we didn't see many dead bodies (they don't play well on television). We don't know what it was like! We think we have a full picture, but we don't, and a little knowledge is a dangerous thing.

Finally, television is by nature a surface medium. It is two-dimensional. It doesn't dig deep; it likes simple issues that can be wrapped up in thirty minutes (or thirty seconds). Everyone is a hero or a villain.

As long as we watched the war on television, it was easy for us to deal with. But when the vets come home and the war becomes more three-dimensional, we'll get a slightly different picture that will be uncomfortable for us. We want the thirty-minute version, and it may be hard to deal with the depth of reality.

The desert and Muslim culture   It was a different world out there, physically and culturally. The desert itself was an enemy to our troops long before they engaged the Iraqis. Sand, hot days, cold nights, fleas, the barrenness of the countryside—all these do a number on an army's morale. They wear you down.

An additional difficulty was the strictness of the Muslim culture. "It was like detox," says one sergeant. "No drinking, no women, nothing."[3] And, especially in the early stages, no Christianity or Judaism—at least not overt forms. This seemed to ease up a bit later.

The behavior restrictions may have been healthy for the Allied forces. Who knows what shape they'd be in after five months of waiting if liquor and drugs were readily available? As one sergeant said: "With all the pressure out there, you wanted to drink but you couldn't."[4]

There may be a reverse culture shock as people return from the gulf. Suddenly confronted with a ready supply of alcohol, drugs, and sex, there may be a tendency to make up for lost time. If you've spent half a year dreaming about your first beer, it might be easy to drink a second, and a third, and. . . .

Threat of chemical and biological weapons The Great Unknown. Whatever it is, it causes fear, and in this war it was Saddam's chemical and biological arsenal. Suddenly, soldiers had gas masks and other protective gear to worry about. Their whole fighting routine was disrupted. This, of course, would only make things more scary.

One medical sergeant tells of a nighttime gas alert in which he fumbled with his mask for a minute or so before getting it on. After he did, he felt a burning sensation on his hands and neck. *"I thought, Oh, God, I didn't make it this time."* It was a false alarm; his senses were playing tricks on him.[5]

A military psychiatrist says that the need to wear chemical protection gear could increase psychiatric casualties by 20 percent. He's talking about battle fatigue. The discomfort of the gear and disruption of routine adds to the basic fear and puts many at risk of breaking down.[6]

Such breakdowns, if they didn't occur during the war, could be "filed away for future use." Fear touches people deeply and could resurface in the future as bad dreams, anxiety, or physical problems.

Involvement of women While not officially in combat roles, women were as close to combat as they've ever been, in a variety of support responsibilities. Of 537,000 United States troops in the Persian Gulf area, more than 33,000 were women. Two women were taken prisoner, three were killed.

It is ironic that this would be the part of the world in which women would take such strides toward equal recognition with men, since the Muslim culture places harsh restrictions on women. One United States servicewoman, in fact, while shopping in Riyadh, was beaten by a member of the Saudi "religious police" for being unveiled.

In any case, this factor has numerous implications. First, we will have many wives returning home to waiting husbands. How will homebound men deal with their war-hero wives? Also, it's likely that the husbands needed emotional support from others but didn't get it (or seek it out). There are many systems in place to help military wives, but military husbands may be slow to ask for them.

New working relationships will have been forged during the war. Some men have been answering to a female superior for the first time in their lives. How will this affect them? Will this change their relationships with their wives? For better or worse?

Of course, the opportunity for improper fraternization was great (especially when the local women were all veiled from head to toe). Doubtless there were many illicit affairs that began in the gulf and may have disastrous effects on many marriages.

The one-sided war   When has a war's outcome been so lopsided? During the entire seven-month operation, the number of United States deaths didn't even reach 200. Iraqi deaths are estimated at up to 100,000. After the first night, the Allies controlled the air. The ground war took all of 100 hours. We've seen telethons that have lasted longer.

The danger is that we can look at the numbers and forget the people on both sides. At some point, some of us may come to grips with the fact that the Allies took six weeks to kill 100,000 Iraqis.

Yes, it was a war. Yes, the Iraqis were the aggressors. Yes, they were guilty of unspeakable atrocities in Kuwait. "Still," as Lance Morrow wrote in *Time,* "killing 100,000 people is a serious thing to do. It is not equivalent to shooting a rabid dog, which is, down deep, what Americans feel the war was all about."[7]

I'm not saying it was wrong to wage this war. I believe it was a just war. Still, we are all in danger of dehumanizing the enemy and ourselves as we deal with these numbers. *The New Republic* editorializes that ''there is a difference between being right and being innocent.''[8] We may have been right in this war, but let's not forget to grieve over the fact that we had to do it. Our celebrations can express thanks for the protection of *our* armies, but we must mourn a bit for our enemy. Maybe we can learn how to do that from some of the returning soldiers who saw their victims up close and personal.

One member of an armored battalion recalled seeing the corpses of Iraqi soldiers. ''I thought, *That's a human being. Yes, he is my enemy and that man wanted to kill me but he is still a human being. I'm sure he had a family somewhere.*''[9]

6

How Bad Is It?

I opened this book with a quick quiz to help you determine your level of post-gulf stress. I want to go back and discuss some of the issues involved—issues that affect you personally.

> A. Who was the person closest to you who was most involved in the Gulf War?
> B. What was the level of danger that person faced?
> D. How much has this person talked to you about his or her experiences?
> E. How much do you think the war has changed this person?

These first four questions establish the level of exposure to the crisis. This affects both those who were in the conflict and their loved ones.

First, we have to understand that *stress is contagious*. It is toxic. It is like a poisonous gas that seeps through an area. It contaminates everyone it touches. Stress spreads through words and glances and changed behavior. If I am stressed by a crisis and you love me, then you are stressed, too.

We must not make light of the anxiety of spouses and other family members back home. Their stress can be as serious as that of the troops themselves. They may not live through the shock of actual combat, but they imagine the scenes many times and replay them in their minds after hearing about them.

We might distinguish three levels of exposure to combat stress:

• **High exposure**   In combat. *Stressors:* Killing others, seeing friends killed and wounded, imminent danger.

• **Medium exposure**   Near combat. *Stressors:* Imminent danger, sight of carnage, dead bodies in war zone, frustration of seeing the action but not being in the action.

• **Low exposure**   In the gulf arena but not in combat zones. *Stressors:* Some danger from missiles, frustration of inactivity, life disruption, general discomfort.

You would think that stress reactions would occur mostly among the high-exposure people, but this is not necessarily so. First, considering the toxicity of stress, we must realize that spouses and friends of the high-exposure combatants are exposed at nearly the same high levels.

Also, do not minimize the importance of frustration among the backups. Research conducted after World War II found that "traumatic war neuroses occur in noncombatant military personnel located in a combat area with a relatively high degree of frequency."[1] In other words, backup *noncombat* personnel experience a lot of stress. This may be a result of that middle-ground experience: wanting to be involved but afraid you might get involved and feeling a bit guilty for feeling afraid. It also may result from the shock of seeing the effects of battle—the wounded soldiers coming back from the lines as well as the enemy casualties in conquered territory.

This also may have to do with different coping mechanisms. Frontline combatants do what they have to do, emotionally speaking. They steel themselves to the horrid experiences they expect to go through. But backup troops may not do the same preparation. The shock of war may take them by surprise. This shock may also be communicated to loved ones.

So the levels of exposure can help us pin down the nature of the stressors, but they do not entirely help us predict how badly a person will be stressed out.

G. How many people did you know who were deployed in the Middle East?

This establishes two things: the level of life disruption and potential exposure to stress. A person with ten dear friends in the gulf had a much better chance of losing one than did a person with two. There was a greater risk of grief, and the person's emotional life is disrupted accordingly. Also, a person with ten friends in the gulf was likely to be inundated with war stories that would convey stress to the person back home. (It's just as if you had ten friends with colds. You're more likely to catch a cold than the person with two ailing friends.)

H. On a scale of 1 to 5, how much was your family life (or individual life) disrupted by the events of the Gulf War?

Life disruption is a major stressor. One of our greatest coping mechanisms in times of stress is to restore a daily routine. When that routine is shaken—by the absence of a family member or an addiction to television news coverage—we are reminded of the problem. This adds to our stress.

I. On a scale of 1 to 5, how worried were you on January 10 (before war broke out but with the approaching deadline) about the outcome of the war?

J. On a scale of 1 to 5, how worried were you on January 17 (the day after war broke out) about the war's outcome?

Shakespeare gave us that great line, "Cowards die a thousand times before their deaths." It's not only cowards. Worriers do, too.

Worry is a way of preparing for disaster. In a way, you anticipate the grieving process. You begin imagining the worst outcome and get ready emotionally for it.

In this case, thankfully, the worst case did not occur. In fact, it was nearly a best-case scenario. Worriers prepared to deal with the stress of grieving, even though most of them didn't have to.

K. From January 16 on, about how much time did you spend, on average, watching television coverage of war events?

More exposure. If you didn't catch the war fever from friends or loved ones in the gulf, you could catch it over the airwaves. It was hard to resist. With *Twin Peaks* in limbo, was there anything more exciting on television than Wolf Blitzer's Pentagon updates or Arthur Kent's Scud reports?

Still, some viewers overdosed on the news. Those worried pilots' wives did the right thing by turning off the sets and trying to get back to their normal lives; too much exposure to television news could overstress you.

L. For how long a period has the Gulf War disrupted your life?

Fatigue is the issue here. Some can withstand great stress for a week or a month, but as the months drag on, the stress wears one down. Many were deployed to the gulf for seven months or more, as the wheels of redeployment turned slowly. Even though the stress of combat itself was mercifully short, the stress of life disruption has eroded many strong families.

      M. How helpful have friends and family been during this time?

The best therapy and the worst stress come from friends and family. A listening ear, embracing arms, a helping hand—these can heal the harried heart. But inappropriate comments, nagging words, and selfish behavior can push a person over the edge. If you have been blessed with supportive loved ones, your chances of weathering this crisis are immeasurably greater.

Why Some Hurt More Than Others

Notice that the quiz merely measured *susceptibility* to post-gulf stress. Actual stress reactions may vary widely. One person may score 65 and be a basket case; another may score 75 and be doing fine. What makes the difference?

A great deal of research has gone into this question. Survivors of dozens of tragedies have been analyzed. Why do some fall apart while others stand firm? Some patterns have emerged.

Inborn resilience   Some people seem to be born with an ability to endure hardship. There is some indication that this resilience follows family lines, so it may be genetic or imparted in childhood.

Previous exposure   This can work both ways. If a person has gone through major crises before—for instance, the battle-hardened vet—he may be strengthened to deal with the current crisis. However, the previous struggles may have worn the person down so the fatigue factor comes into play. The person may cry, "I've had enough. I can't take anymore!" This is especially true if there's something unique or surprising about the current stressor. It may find a "chink in the armor" of the most hardened person.

Point in individual development Each of us is in a certain trajectory of growth. We are learning things, assimilating things we've learned, or questioning things. A stressful crisis can push us further along or knock us back; it depends where we are. As a chaplain, I am particularly aware of how tragedies affect people's faith in God. Some find their faith strengthened. They learn to trust God in this hard time. Others "lose" their faith in times like this. "How could God let this happen?" It all depends on where a person is in his faith development and what image he has of God. Reports from the gulf indicate that there was a lot of turning *to* God. We tend not to hear of those who turn *away from* God, but I'm sure this happened, too.

Preexisting problems If you were neurotic before the war, you will probably be more so afterward. If your marriage was falling apart, seven months in the desert sand won't help much. (Although it might. Stranger things have happened.)

In the early stages of the war, navy psychiatrist and rear admiral Richard I. Ridenour reported few mental health problems among the deployed troops. "Some of the people showing symptoms of clinical depression," he said, "probably would have been depressed wherever they were."[2]

Many marital struggles were reported as troops returned home. But a common refrain is heard: "They were in trouble before Daddy left," says one observant child-care worker.[3]

Trauma is a magnifying glass. It will magnify your problems, find your weakest point, and make it weaker.

Social supports We have touched on this already. Friends and family can help or hurt, but it goes beyond this. Where do you go when you need help? If you have a network of friends you can rely on, great. If you have a church or synagogue or social group that can offer assistance, wonderful. If you have a trusted counselor, use him or her. Those without such social supports can be wrecked by a trauma like this war.

Sociocultural context What does society think of your situation? So far, with this war, this factor has been positive. (A far cry from the Vietnam situation.) It was a popular war, and there seems to be an outpouring of support for its participants. But watch out for developments in the next year. World events may turn our opinions around. The news media will tire of the gulf vets and move on to other celebrities. The support might dry up while you still need it. It will be harder to recover from this crisis if American society is not behind you.

How stressed are you by this war? How stressed are those around you? Read on for more understanding of the needs we're all facing and how to deal with them.

7

Nostalgia: War Trauma Through the Ages

During the Civil War, soldiers were found wandering the battlefield, disoriented, seemingly unaware of the conflict around them. The medics called this "nostalgia," from the Greek words for "the pain of returning home." In their minds, at least, these Yanks and Rebs had blocked out the savage fury of war and had returned to their peaceful homes.

In World War I, the experts called this "shell shock." They figured that the blasts of artillery had battered the ear and brain of the baffled soldier. That was when a new strategy for treatment was pioneered.

In the new method, developed by Dr. Thomas Salmon of New York, shell-shocked soldiers were not sent home to recover. They were merely removed from the front lines—in fact, later studies showed that recovery was better when they were still within earshot of battle sounds. It was expected that, after a few days of rest, they could return to battle. Seventy to eighty percent did.

Obviously, this worked out well for the armed forces. They were essentially "recycling" their mentally wounded troops. But studies have shown that this method was best for the soldier's long-term recovery as well. Many who were sent home faced numerous post-traumatic problems—bad dreams, continuing fear of loud noises, and a number of guilt-related woes, to name a few. But those who were rested and returned to battle fared better. (This was confirmed by Israeli researchers in the wake of the Yom Kippur War of 1973. Israel evacuated its stressed soldiers to civilian hospitals, resulting in virtually no return to action and chronic disability thereafter.)

This may be like the child who nearly drowns and decides never to swim again. The wise parent urges the child to return to the water soon, after a brief time away, to exorcise those fears. So the soldier who is overwhelmed in battle may be helped more by urging than by coddling. After a suitable rest, he may be ready for battle again. Without a return to action, the fears may fester forever.

So goes the theory of this treatment method, which became known as "PIE"—Proximity, Immediacy, Expectation. Keep the patient close to the battlefield but pull him out of action right away, yet make sure he expects to go back to the lines. One additional benefit of this method is that the soldier can maintain contact with his unit. The personal relations and group morale can assist recovery considerably.

The wisdom gleaned in World War I was forgotten in the early days of World War II. Now they were calling the problem "combat fatigue" or "combat exhaustion." They tended to whisk suffering soldiers back home immediately. Most of these never returned to action.

Later in that war, and in the Korean War, officials began to study the problem. They learned that the number of "stress-related reactions" (cases of combat fatigue) was directly related to the number of soldiers physically wounded. This makes sense, since fiercer fighting would bring about more casualties of both body and mind. But a ratio of one (mental) to three (physical) seemed to apply.

The number of combat fatigue cases also corresponded to the length of time troops were in combat. A U-shaped pattern emerged. In the first few days of combat, many would succumb, perhaps surprised by the ferocity of the action. But then the soldiers got used to battle (or the most susceptible ones were weeded out), and there were fewer cases. Yet, as the battle wore on, exhaustion would set in, and the incidence of combat fatigue would rise.

Such studies allowed authorities to set policies of troop rotation to lessen the problem. During the Vietnam conflict, the military was well prepared to deal with combat stress. In the early period of that war, relatively few soldiers had to return home for psychiatric reasons. But there were new stressors in Vietnam.

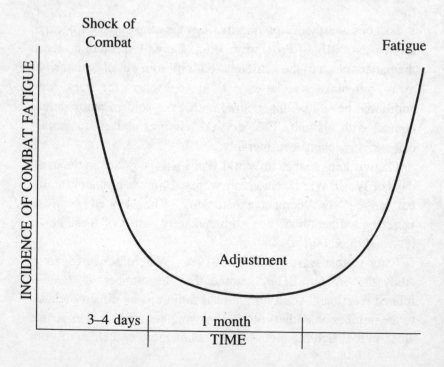

The guerrilla nature of the war had to wear down the troops. Drug abuse and low morale have also been blamed.

As a result, the number of combat fatigue cases soared, with lasting effects—for the individual soldiers and for society at large. Thanks to movies such as *Rambo, Coming Home,* and *Born on the Fourth of July,* the shell-shocked Vietnam vet has become a symbol in our culture. According to the stereotype, this person is a loner, responsive only to other vets, unable to concentrate on meaningful activity, angry, self-pitying, perhaps a drug user.

Certainly, there are thousands of well-adjusted Vietnam vets in our society, but this stereotype presents us with a few truths we find hard to ignore. War hurts people. And even if they make it through the battle physically unscathed, the stress of the conflict can wreak havoc on their minds.

In the period after Vietnam, in the two decades of relative peace, our national attention was focused on the aftermath of combat stress. Numerous studies have been conducted on *post-traumatic problems.* How does combat fatigue affect a soldier years after the trauma of battle? What symptoms affect him? How can we help him—and his loved ones—cope?

Already, we have referred to several different sorts of "stress disorders" (the term most recently in vogue). It would help to make some distinctions.

1. Shock.   This is the beginning of that U-shaped curve. In battle, the initial stress—of being in danger, of seeing a friend die, of caring for a seriously wounded comrade, of killing someone else—can overwhelm a person.

In the Gulf conflict, the potential for shock was considerable. Our armed forces were packed with reservists and National Guard units. And, face it, even the regular units included many who had never anticipated actually being in a war. They had signed up to learn a trade or get a scholarship—to be all that they could be.

The actions of Saddam Hussein and the responses of George Bush threw such people into an unexpected whirlwind of activity. But even the months of preparation in the desert sands could not have fully prepared them for the shock of battle.

2. Fatigue. This is the second prong of that U-shaped curve. After about a month of combat, soldiers get sick and tired of it, literally. Often there are simple life-style factors involved, such as lack of proper food or sleep. (Interestingly, this was one major strategy of the Allies against Hussein's Republican Guard—constant bombardment to inhibit sleep, while waiting for the embargo to starve them out.)

But fatigue can also result merely from the constancy of battle stress. Spend too much time dodging grenades or hearing bullets whiz past your head, and you go a bit crazy.

The actual conflict in the gulf lasted such a short time that battle fatigue was not a problem. But something very close to it was: we might call it "readiness fatigue."

We had suddenly deployed some 530,000 troops to a desert area for an uncertain amount of time. Consider the stressors involved.

Separation from family. Remember that many of these families were not expecting such separation. It was a sudden upheaval. The families back home were stressed, and the troops in the gulf were stressed by worrying about what was happening at home.

Physical discomfort. It was hot. Even in cooler climates, army life is no picnic. But Desert Shield/Storm was a hot, gritty operation.

Culture shock. In the Muslim culture of Saudi Arabia, many of the accoutrements of normal American life—music, films, sexual relations for some, religious observances for others—were inappropriate. For many servicepeople, Desert Shield was like going to a very strict religious school—of a different religion!

Even the driving patterns were unfamiliar to American troops.

Note that many of the pre-war casualties were victims of traffic accidents.

Boredom. Many returnees have cited boredom as a major foe, even after the war began. Only a portion of our troops actually saw action. The others mostly played cards and watched videos. Boredom is a different kind of stressor. It can create great anxiety, especially in conjunction with other factors.

Uncertainty of future. Would we go to war? If so, what kind of war would it be? How strong was Iraq? Would they use chemical weapons? How long would the war last?

The January 15 deadline gave a certain fixed point in a waffling world. But the questions still abounded. The soldiers—and their families back home—could not plan for the future. They had no idea what that would hold. This was made worse by changing rotation policies. Some who expected to leave the gulf area after a certain period were not allowed to. This created some resentment and additional uncertainty.

These and other factors combined to create stress of varying intensity.

One reservist sent regular reports to a hometown weekly newspaper, *The Voice,* in New Baltimore, Michigan. In his first letter, dated October 11, 1990, Dick Runels wrote:

> . . . this is a sand-covered, flea-infested, hot, smelly, congested—did I mention hot?—very basic tent/hooch city that has been force-grown in a hurry to deal with a situation nobody really knows about or knows how it will turn out.
>
> Regardless of the interviews given, we are not all happy to be here, nor did we expect to be here. And we can't wait to get home. . . .

In his second report, dated October 27, we see the stress factors building.

It's finally set in—reality, that is. Now almost everyone realizes that, yes, we are going to be here ninety days or more. For some it is a hard fact to face that Thanksgiving, probably Christmas, maybe even New Year's will be spent right here, in the sand. . . .

The rumor mill works overtime. We're rotating on schedule; we're rotating before Thanksgiving; war will begin October 15, October 17, November 10, December 24 (pick a date). . . . The basic truth is that nobody knows what is going on. When we get home, we get home. . . .

Like the GIs at the front, boredom and uncertainty are the leading feelings here. When is something going to happen? *Is* something going to happen? What will happen to me if something *does* happen? If we knew, it would be much easier. . . .

Runels's third letter, November 4, expressed concerns, since he had received "very depressing news about how our dependents back home are being treated." False hopes, uncertain expectations, unfounded rumors were all having their dismal effects. "Every night someone calls home and finds his wife in tears because of some rumor she's heard."

His fourth and final letter, November 22, complained about military censorship and the extension of stay in Saudi Arabia.

Morale at Mirage [his camp] is practically nonexistent. Having been extended ninety days more has *everyone* terminally bummed. It was just getting easy to accept the ninety days, then on "hump day," the halfway point, zowie! We get it right between the eyes. Ninety more with the possibility of 180 more on top of that![1]

Other reports have confirmed that these feelings of uncertainty were tormenting the deployed soldiers. Such feelings are bound to leave a residue of anxiety, even after the war is over.

3. Depression. If new recruits are the most susceptible to shock and combat fatigue, what happens to battle-hardened vets? They often suffer from symptoms of depression.

Why? An old Vietnam catchphrase may help explain it: "It don't mean nuthin'." Your buddy gets blown away—keep going, it don't mean nuthin'. You have to torch a village of women and children to flush out the VC—keep going, it don't mean nuthin'. In the heat of battle, this is a survival tactic. If you stop to consider the meaning of every human life involved, you'll never get the job done. The only way to save yourself from the stress of battle shock or fatigue is to deny the meaning of what is happening.

That gets you through the day. But what happens the next day, or the next week, or the next year? You have effectively denied the meaning of life. So what is the meaning of *your* life? The sense of meaninglessness leads to depression.

This is especially prevalent among career soldiers, those who have risen to "middle management" ranks. (This is sometimes called the "old sergeant syndrome.") Adding to the meaninglessness is that the person's old buddies, the unit he started with, have left the service or been reassigned. So there is no social support. The "old sergeant" is alone, doing a job without meaning.

It is generally agreed that the Vietnam War had huge questions of meaning, anyway. So it is not surprising that depression was a common reaction to the stress. But, if anything, the Gulf conflict may have *cured* the depression of some career officers. Here was a war with meaning. All along the chain of command, people were not just doing their jobs, they were participating in a moral judgment on an evil tyrant. Besides that, they were restoring America's image in the world. They were atoning for the sins and errors of Vietnam.

The depression, if it comes, may come later. With Hussein retaining power, and with his mistreatment of the Kurds, new questions are arising about the meaning of this conflict. But, for

the moment, most of those "old sergeants" have been rejuve-
nated.

4. Delayed reactions. Even if they don't suffer shell shock
during a conflict, many soldiers experience symptoms of post-
traumatic stress upon their return home or later in life.

These are the problems this book is addressing. On top of the
physical and mental difficulties that may result from this delayed
response, a variety of interpersonal and economic problems may
add stress. A harsh spiral may result, as the classic symptoms of
post-traumatic stress disorder (PTSD) put stress on the social and
economic environment of the returning vet. This erodes the support the vet needs to overcome the physical and mental problems.

As a hypothetical example, John comes home from the gulf
after flying many successful bombing missions. A few months
after his return, he begins having dreams of the people his bombs
landed on. He has one especially vivid image of people running
away from a bomb he has dropped. These dreams make it difficult for him to sleep—and for his wife to sleep. This results in
greater irritability for both. They've been having more fights
lately.

The dreams by themselves are not much to worry about. They
are normal stress reactions. But the weakening marriage may be
harder to shore up. Without the loving support of his wife, John's
symptoms may worsen, which will put even greater stress on the
marriage. And so on.

Or look at Frank, an activated reservist who secretly feels bad
because he made a crucial error in the ground campaign that put
his unit in danger. As it turned out, the enemy never picked up on
the error and the unit survived. But Frank keeps replaying the
situation in his mind, worrying about what might have happened.
This keeps him from concentrating.

When Frank gets back to his stateside job as a computer pro-
grammer, his inability to focus on his work makes his produc-

tivity decline. This makes him feel even worse about himself. Eventually, he loses his job, which puts a strain on his marriage. His lack of focus in finding a new job makes his wife accuse him of laziness. For a while, she is the major wage earner in the home, which he finds objectionable but can do nothing about. His self-image plummets even further.

"What is wrong with you!" Frank's wife finally screams. Well, nothing much. Really, Frank's problem is nothing that some wise counseling couldn't help. But by now there are huge economic and marital issues that complicate the problem. With success at work and support from his wife, Frank could put his battlefield blunder behind him. But the downward spiral has made it harder to deal with.

An Easy War?

The perception continues that this was an "easy" war, that U.S. forces sustained few casualties and therefore we can all feel pretty good about Desert Storm. It was not another Vietnam. In fact, it was the pill we needed to forget Vietnam.

I am not arguing the politics of the matter. Should we have been there or not? Should we have gone further to wipe out Saddam's power? Other writers can debate these points.

But I am concerned about this idea we have of painless conflict. There is no such thing. The TV cameras may have hidden the dead bodies from our view. The vast majority of casualties were Iraqi and therefore they mattered less to us. More Americans than we'd care to admit got limbs blown off by land mines, yet their cries have been drowned out by the victory marches.

And what we can't count yet are the many who will yet suffer— emotionally and psychologically—from their gulf involvement. Post-traumatic stress disorder may surface a year or more after the initial events that trigger it. Even if someone is not clinically diagnosed with PTSD, he or she may be suffering from some of its symptoms.

Fortunately, this hasn't been another Vietnam—*so far*. The military, social, and psychological difficulties of that conflict have not been matched by this one. But we can't afford to ignore the problems that will arise after Desert Storm. If we do, then the private agony of thousands of Vietnam vets will have taught us little.

8

Dealing With Loss

"Don't forget about all the people that didn't come home," pleads Karen Bnosky. An army captain herself, this twenty-six-year-old lost her husband, Lieutenant Jeffrey Bnosky, in a pre-combat accident. Yes, she says, "casualties are low. But to those of us who were affected by the casualties, it was too many."

The two had separate assignments in Saudi Arabia. After two and a half months apart, they managed to rendezvous near Dhahran January 11.

"On their last night together," reports *USA Today*, "sitting outside a tent on a picnic table, they each took off their gold bands and exchanged wedding vows again. Then it was time for him to leave. . . ."[1]

Four hours later, Karen was praying. "I felt a real peace inside," she says. "God wouldn't give me anything I couldn't handle."

At that same moment, Jeffrey was killed in a jeep accident. His bent wedding band was returned to Karen.

"There's going to be a lot of homecomings," she says, "but my husband is not coming home."

Casualties from the gulf seem to carry an extra weight for their mourners because they are so rare. The general consensus in the U.S. is that this was a painless war. Don't tell that to Karen Bnosky or to the families of the twenty-eight people killed when the Scud missile hit their barracks February 25. Their loss is as great as any during Vietnam or Korea or World War II. And maybe it's greater, because *no one wants to hear about it.* With our nation reveling in a picture-perfect outcome, we don't want mourning families to spoil the view.

But we must not ignore them. Their lives are shattered. Their hopes and dreams are dashed. Karen could tell you how Jeffrey was going to leave the service in June and spend some time fishing, hunting, and riding a mountain bike near their Missouri home. Now her plans are radically altered.

Any major loss we undergo involves damage to four basic assumptions we hold. These are those first-floor ideas we've already talked about, the ways we think the world ought to operate.

Invulnerability

"Bad things should never happen to me."

We seldom put it so baldly, but most of us live our lives like this. We're talking about *really* bad things, now. We get parking tickets and lose our keys and get passed over for promotions at work. But catastrophes happen to other people. They don't touch us.

One researcher has found that people tend to overestimate the positive things that might happen to them *and underestimate the likelihood of experiencing negative events.* We live in a land of optimists. Not that we assume we will always be happy, but we do tilt our expectations toward the positive side.

This is especially true of young people. We mature as we mature. Many older folks have had to face numerous deaths in their families, perhaps other crises as well. But teenagers, and even those in their twenties (which includes the bulk of people involved in the Gulf conflict), still imagine that they are untouchable. We see this in the way this generation faces (or refuses to face) the AIDS crisis. Many continue in drug use and dangerous sexual activity, convinced that "it won't happen to me." We are Superman. Bullets bounce off us. Or so we imagine, until one bullet gets through.

This attitude leaves us totally unprepared for crisis. Disasters blindside us. Hard times *do* happen, threatening our carefully preserved sense of invulnerability. Then we are immobilized.

I still remember counseling people in the Dallas–Fort Worth Hilton who were emotionally incapacitated by the Delta crash. They had lost daughters and sons, wives and husbands. Disaster had struck, and they didn't know how to handle it. Their veneer of invulnerability had been penetrated. They were victims, utterly and thoroughly at the mercy of things beyond their control.

Rationality

"The world should make sense."

At the very core of our being, most of us believe the world runs according to logical principles. There should be reasons for the things that happen.

We gain a certain control of our world as we understand it. We gain confidence from knowing that the world works a certain way, and if it doesn't, we know why. We need answers for the events around us.

"If I were a better person, my husband wouldn't have died in that crash. God was trying to teach me a lesson."

We often create intricate schemes, severely judgmental of ourselves or others, in order to regain rational control over disastrous events.

"I think God let my wife die because He knew our marriage would only get worse if she had lived. We had been having more arguments lately. Maybe God knew we were headed for a painful divorce anyway."

When we are forced to face difficult questions, we develop *myths* to answer them. These myths are not necessarily false—in fact, they usually have grains of truth in them. We are using the classic definition of *myth,* not as a falsehood but as "an attempt to answer basic questions."

After the Delta crash, a flight attendant came up to me, identifying herself as a Christian. "I know why the crash happened," she said. She went to explain something that had been discovered while the identities of victims were checked against the passenger list. One businessman on board was traveling with a secretary who was using his wife's name. They were obviously sneaking off for some illicit tryst. That, the flight attendant said, was why God let this plane crash—to punish this lustful couple.

That was her myth. She could maintain her belief in a righteous but loving God by blaming these sinners for the tragedy. But I couldn't help wondering: Is that the kind of God we have, one who would kill 137 people to punish one man? Her myth caused more problems than it solved.

But, like most crisis myths, hers was really not an intellectual answer. It was an emotional struggle to regain some rational control over confusing events. She was reaching for anything to quiet her doubts.

On the other side of the spectrum, I was astonished to see that another chaplain was quoted in the Dallas papers as having said that God had "nothing to do with" the Delta crash. This was his attempt, I suppose, to bolster people's faith in a loving God.

But this view has serious implications. Do we really want to say our God has no control over what happens in the world? Unfortunately, this is a popular view among clerics who wrestle with life's complexities. God becomes the benevolent Watchmaker in the sky who winds up His creation and watches it tick—or drifts off to sleep as the watch runs down. This myth also falls short.

I'm tempted to begin a theological debate at this point, but I'll declare a stalemate from the outset. The simple fact is that there are some things in life we just can't understand. This in itself is bothersome because there are many things we *can* understand. There is a certain logic to the way we are made and the way the universe is made. I believe God wants us to use our minds to understand many things about Him. But there will always be those things that confuse. We just have to shrug sometimes and say, "I don't know why this happened. It just happened."

For those of us with a deep-rooted assumption of rationality, that is very hard to do.

Morality

"People get what they deserve."

This may be a uniquely American (or "Western") assumption. We live in a society built on justice and fair treatment. We have been spared the whims of tyrants. Our culture is meritocratic—the people who merit leadership positions get them—or so we like to think. Good, hardworking people are rewarded. Lazy people are punished. Maybe it goes back to the Puritan work ethic. Or maybe it's the pioneer spirit of the settlers. Or perhaps it's turn-of-the-century individualism. There are good guys and bad guys, hard workers and lazy bums, white hats and black hats. And the good guy walks off into the sunset with the girl.

(Apologies if that seems sexist to you. It is. The fact is that meritocracy has always left out women.)

When we carry this out to its logical extremes, we see the faults of this assumption. People *don't* always get what they deserve. Some work hard and get very little. We tend to recognize this fact on the surface, but deep down we still count on a basic justice in the universe.

What do we say when a personal tragedy strikes? ''What did I do to deserve this?''

We usually feel as if we have a contract with God (or with whoever is running the universe).

What we give: decent behavior; love of family; possibly practice of a religion.

What we get: a life of at least seventy years; generally good health; children who grow into adults and care for us in our old age; a decent job with decent pay; enjoyable relationships with friends.

Sorry to say, there is no such contract. Ask Job. In the biblical story, he was ''blameless and upright; he feared God and shunned evil'' (Job 1:1). What happened? He lost his savings, his kids were kidnapped by terrorists, his wife left him, and he contracted a painful disease.

The truth is this: Bad things often happen to good people and good things happen to bad people. Ask Asaph, who wrote Psalm 73. We like to dawdle in the green pastures of Psalm 23, but fifty chapters later, the psalmist complains about the ''prosperity of the wicked.''

> They have no struggles;
>   their bodies are healthy and strong.
> They are free from the burdens common to man;
>   they are not plagued by human ills. . . .
> This is what the wicked are like—
>   always carefree, they increase in wealth.
>
> Psalm 73:3, 4, 12

The writer goes on to accuse God of reneging on their implied contract:

Surely in vain have I kept my heart pure;
    in vain have I washed my hands in innocence.
All day long I have been plagued;
    I have been punished every morning.

                                          Psalm 73:13, 14

We have difficulty grasping this. Our belief in a just universe runs very deep. Tragedies seem unfair. Why would a good, loving husband like Jeffrey Bnosky be taken from his wife? In the very moment that she prays for peace of mind—and gets it ("God wouldn't give me anything I couldn't handle")—his life is snatched away. And at this writing, Saddam Hussein is still walking free in Baghdad, still enjoying the privileges of power.

This is wrong, we feel. It violates all the principles of justice. The world is no longer a fair place. And God—if He is in control—is a criminal.

Once again, our assumptions are shaken. We have lost not only a friend, a darling, a child, a comrade but also a bit of what we believe in.

Identity

"I'm Bill's wife."
"I'm Sarah's father."
"I'm the mother of three."
"Jennifer and I are going to be man and wife."

We are so connected to the people we love that part of our identity is wrapped up in them. We define ourselves by our relationships. So when a tragedy takes someone away, we have to redefine ourselves.

If Bill is killed in the ground war against Iraq, what does his wife say? "I'm Bill's widow?" "I was Bill's wife?" We hope that she can discover her own name and recast her identity—to "find herself." But that takes work. And it hurts. A piece of her identity is gone.

Say the "mother of three" loses one son in the gulf. When people ask how many children she has (and they *always* do), what does she say? Two? Three—two here, one in heaven?

What if "Jennifer" or "Sarah" dies in a desert accident? How does her fiancé or father define himself now?

Something dies in us when a loved one dies. We don't know who we are anymore.

Sometimes we can lose something else, too: our ability to invest our lives in others. We carry a residual fear that *this will happen again*. "I was so badly wounded by this loss, I never want to go through that again. So I will never again identify so thoroughly with someone else."

That can result in wall-building. We shut ourselves off from other relationships, even from those who can help us. You see, it is not wrong to identify with others. In fact, it is practically necessary. In order to benefit from intimate relationships, we must commit ourselves to them. That requires a certain investment, a sharing of our inner selves. And that's dangerous. Good, but dangerous. It opens us up to the pain of loss.

A person once burned by losing a loved one may decide not to take those interpersonal risks again.

These four assumptions are not totally off base. There is a measure of truth in each. We can find a point of equilibrium in each matter.

We can legitimately recognize that we have, *so far,* been invulnerable to disaster (if that is the case) and be thankful for that. In fact, it is possible to go too far the other way and fret constantly about one's vulnerability.

Shortly after the Delta crash, I realized I was feeling skittish about flying. The close involvement with families of crash victims had infected me with a certain fear of vulnerability. I asked my commander to give me an assignment that would require some flight time. I was seeking an equilibrium. My sense of invulnerability had been shattered; I was now all too aware how vulnerable an aircraft is. I needed to calm my fears by getting a reasonable reckoning of the risks involved.

Similarly, it is proper to recognize a certain degree of rationality and even justice in the universe. One can go too far in denying all reason. Some philosophers have chosen to go that route. A kind of despair results. I believe that God does rule the universe, but according to His own reasoning, which frequently goes beyond my own.

One could become bitter about the lack of justice in the universe. Many have. Equilibrium is reached as we recognize that our actions do have consequences; *to some extent,* there is earthly advantage to good behavior, though these rewards are limited. As a Christian I believe God's justice will not be finalized until the next world. Even then, it will be tempered with grace—we will get many rewards we *don't* deserve.

The same pattern applies to identity. Those who wrap themselves up entirely in a spouse or parent or child are destined for trouble. If Bill's wife is *only* Bill's wife, and has no other identity, she will face serious problems when Bill dies. And yet, as we have said, a certain amount of identification with others is necessary. It's a chance we have to take.

With any loss, these assumptions will be shaken. The healthy person will grow back to an equilibrium point, but this will take time. There will be bitterness, anger, questioning, fear, or identity problems in the meantime. These are normal stopovers on the flight back to wholeness.

9

On the Balance Beam

Once we examine our basic assumptions and see how thoroughly a catastrophe can shatter them, we recognize how "iffy" our lives are. Our plans, our relationships, our livelihood all depend on the absence of catastrophe. *If* the world doesn't blow up, *if* I don't get run over by a truck, *if* I don't lose my job, I can meet you for lunch next Thursday.

Of course, we can't live like that. Start talking that way, and soon you won't have any friends to meet for lunch. Yet those issues need to enter our minds occasionally, just to remind us what's really important.

Years ago, there was a popular poster that cheerily declared, "Today is the first day of the rest of your life." But let's turn that around: "Today is the last day of your life so far." Depressing, isn't it?

Some sage once suggested: "Live each day as if it were your last." What difference would that make? For some, that's a license to live it up. "Eat, drink, and be merry, for tomorrow we die." For others, it's a call to invest their lives in meaningful relationships and service to others.

The thousands of reservists and National Guardsmen who faced the possibility of deployment in the gulf (including me) know this "last day" existence all too well. For about six months beginning August 2, 1990, we all had to make tentative plans. We never knew when orders might come, sending us halfway around the world. It was a tense time, because we recognized that deployment, even in backup roles, might mean death (especially with the possibility of chemical warfare). Even those who could handle the anxiety found that the details of their lives became much more important in those difficult days.

Halfway through my dealings with the Delta crash, I went back home to get some fresh clothes. It had been a grueling week for me, as I tended the needs of hundreds of distraught people. Too many parents were grieving the loss of their children, regretting things they had said or hadn't said. Too many children were trying to cope with the loss of parents from whom they had never really received approval. I was exhausted.

Arriving home late at night, I went to kneel by the beds of each of my three kids. "Dear God," I begged, "may I never again leave this house without telling my kids how much I love them."

I wish I could say that I've been true to that commitment, but I haven't, not entirely. The Delta tragedy reminded me how short life can be. It made me question my assumptions, which caused me some anxiety, but it also helped me get some priorities straight.

Keeping Our Balance

We live on a balance beam. At any moment we can fall off into careless confidence or paralyzing fear. A catastrophe such as war can knock us off the beam, but the healing process slowly lifts us back up.

Interestingly, the most common symptoms of post-traumatic stress illustrate that off-balance behavior.

Some Symptoms of Post-Traumatic Stress

Too much sleep	Too little sleep
Works constantly	Finds it hard to work
Great sexual desire	Little or no sexual desire
Needs to be with people all the time	Withdraws from people

Sleep, work, sex, socializing—all perfectly natural, normal things. In our normal lives, we find a point of moderation for each of them, but the shock of war or personal loss throws us into extremes. We need to find our balance again.

With that background, we want to look at specific types of losses that people are dealing with in the aftermath of the Gulf War. How can we find our balance and get back on that beam?

Death

With the death of a loved one, our first reaction is simple grief: The deceased person is missed; we are sorry not to enjoy his or her company. In extreme situations, the griever decides that life is simply not worth living without the deceased person. But, as we pass through the various stages of grief, we eventually get used to not having the person around. Other factors can complicate the grieving process.

There are usually regrets, things said or not said, things done or not done. "I wish I had told him I loved him." "I wish we hadn't had that silly argument." "We never did go to a ball game, like we promised." "Why didn't we spend more time together?" In extreme forms, the regrets turn to guilt. For a while, such grievers can be overattentive to other friends. They may linger over each good-bye, afraid that it might be the last, or they may clam up, afraid to say anything they might regret later.

Sometimes regret can turn to self-blame. "If I hadn't com-

plained about money so much, he wouldn't have joined the reserves." "He was probably thinking about me when he made
that fatal error."

Soldiers often blame themselves when a buddy gets killed. "If
I were paying more attention. . . ." "If I had warned him. . . ."
"If I had led the unit the other way. . . ." The sad fact is that this
is often true; soldiers do depend on one another and their leaders.
Mistakes are made, jeopardizing others. Friendly fire took sev-
eral lives during this conflict. It's a fact of war.

In extreme forms, self-blame can seriously damage our self-
image. The off-balance behavior could be a crippling lack of
confidence or bravado by which the person tries to prove himself.

Self-blame is especially likely in the aftermath of the Gulf
War, where no one was supposed to get killed (and relatively few
did). Casualties were the exception rather than the rule. There is
no powerful enemy to blame, so soldiers may feel that every
death was due to an error, not just the normal cost of doing battle.

Closely related to this is survivor guilt. "Why did I deserve to
live while he died?" This is also common among soldiers, but
it's not tied to specific actions. It's just a vague feeling of injustice, where you feel you're contributing to the injustice by remaining alive while better people died.

Extreme cases of survivor guilt result in a loss of personal
identity, preoccupation with the deceased person, constant attention to what he or she would say or do. A fellow soldier might
seek to visit the home of the deceased soldier, paying his "debt"
by honoring the loved ones of the fallen comrade.

Often the blame is directed outward. "George Bush had no
right to send the troops over there in the first place." "The
commanding officer should have known better than to send Joe's
unit into that bunker. He just wanted to get the glory." Grief-
inspired anger can encourage all sorts of hateful thoughts, resulting in bitterness or severed relationships.

Such anger can be woven into the particular mythology surrounding each war casualty. When an army airborne charter crashed in Gander, Newfoundland, in 1985, many grieving wives were convinced that army penny-pinching was to blame. "If they had paid the money to use a more reliable plane, it wouldn't have crashed." The argument is probably not valid, but it did serve as a way of casting blame. This provided some sense of meaning to an otherwise senseless disaster.

This relentless search for meaning is another symptom of post-war grief. As we have already said, people like to think that life is rational, that everything happens for a reason, but the events of war can rattle that assumption.

This is especially true of this war. While the overall need for action in the gulf was widely accepted, granting a certain meaning to the war, a large percentage of the American casualties seemed to have little to do with combat.

What meaning do we attach to the deaths of the several who were killed in precombat traffic accidents? How did the deaths of the twenty-eight killed in their barracks by a Scud missile help the war effort? How we do explain those who were killed by friendly fire in the ground war? What about those killed in post-combat minesweeping?

The official line is that each of these deceased soldiers is a hero killed in the faithful service of our country. This is true, but the families of these heroes have nagging doubts. The deaths of their loved ones seem unnecessary and senseless.

These grievers can go off balance by entering an existential depression where there is no meaning to anything. Or they can decide to give meaning to the death by pouring their lives into some new cause. They'll go to seminary, join the Peace Corps, make the world a better place—all inspired by the sacrifice of their loved one. These may be fine actions, but a person must do such things for herself, not in a desperate attempt to give meaning to a casualty of war.

Injury

What of those who were shot in this war or lost a limb to a land mine? Here again, the casualties were mercifully few. Still, there are some returning from the gulf in wheelchairs or on crutches, and their lives have been forever changed.

Injured veterans face many of the same issues as families of the deceased. There is often regret, bitterness, blame, a search for meaning. They sustained a loss in the Arabian desert; they lost their wholeness. They, too, must go through a grieving process.

First, their sense of invulnerability has been shattered. They got hit! This may manifest itself in off-balance behavior such as extreme fear or extreme cockiness, or perhaps a combination of the two.

Second, the injured vet is usually thrown into uncertainty. Will he recover? How fully? What medical care is necessary? How normal can his life become? How will people react to him? Will he be able to return to his job? How will this affect his marriage? How will his children respond?

Denial is common at this stage—and often healthy. No matter what the doctor's prognosis, the vet may insist that he *will* recover through persistence and hard work. Hollywood loves these stories, where the vet fights back from a crippling injury to beat the odds and play basketball once more, but the fact is that the doctors are usually right.

Yet denial serves a healthy function. Few people can psychologically embrace full-blown reality on the spot. Denial buffers the impact of hard truth. It buys us time. Eventually, the vet will attain a realistic outlook and begin to put his life back together.

At that point, issues of identity arise. With basic matters such as career and family up in the air, how does the injured vet see himself? He's different from the guy who went off to war. His hopes and dreams must undergo a major overhaul. He cannot do some things he used to do. Who is he, anyway? There is a great deal of work to be done, as he finds out what he *can* do and reorders his expectations.

Anger is another natural outgrowth of a war injury. Blame the president, blame the army, blame Hussein, blame your sergeant, blame yourself. This is another one of those classic "stages of grief," a way station on the road to acceptance. Unfortunately, many get stuck here and stew in their bitterness for the rest of their lives.

Numerous family issues must also be recognized. Children must learn to see their father differently. He used to play catch with them or carry them to bed. Now he can't. The wife has to shoulder new responsibilities. The balance of power in the home shifts. Research has shown that role reversals are not uncommon in marriages of injured veterans.[1] Since the wife can do more things, she begins to take charge. She may assume the main role in disciplining the kids. This may all work out well, if there is communication and acceptance. But if the family members harbor bitterness, self-pity, or unspoken expectations, there could be trouble. The family may also take too much care of the injured vet, fostering a sense of dependency and helplessness.

All along, the injured vet is probably feeling paradoxical emotions. He's a hero! He has a Purple Heart to prove it. He can be justifiably proud of his service in the war. But life is really hard when you're disabled. Every day, he wonders what his life would be like if he hadn't gone, hadn't served, hadn't been a hero. And so he teeters between pride and self-pity.

His family feels the same mix of emotions. Dad's a hero! Children are proud as they wave the flags on Veteran's Day. But Johnny's dad took him canoeing; why can't mine? Life is hard for them, too. A wife may find that her attraction to her injured husband has declined. He may be disfigured, or just incapable. There may be sexual difficulties, as well. She feels pride in him, pity for him, but she sometimes wishes she had a different life— this one is just too tough.

The family equilibrium has gone awry. Together, they need to find a new balance.

Loss of Innocence

One pilot told me of the shock of seeing faces below him. He had already flown several successful bombing sorties. On this one, he soared over an Iraqi ship in the gulf. Looking down, he saw men on the ship—men like him, serving their country. The men saw the plummeting bombs and ran for cover. Moments later, the ship exploded.

Those faces still haunt that pilot. "I killed those people," he tells himself. "I made them die."

Up to that point, war was something like a video game. Push the buttons, drop the bombs, teach that tyrant a lesson. It was all so technological, so antiseptic. But there were real people at the other end of those bombs. War is an ugly business, and no amount of technology can erase that fact.

That pilot lost something in the air above the gulf: He lost his innocence. He entered the gritty world of no easy answers and was forced to find his own place in that world.

For those of us who watched it on CNN, the war seemed easy. It was a chess match. We took their knights and chased their pawns to Basra. But not all the pawns surrendered. Imagine the eighteen-year-old recruit who storms a bunker and finds the remains of an Iraqi soldier he has shot. Hooray! It's a victory! But imagine him checking the guy's wallet and finding pictures of his children. The boy realizes he has killed another human being, a father, a husband. Something inside him wants to scream, but he can't. There's another bunker to storm, another Iraqi to shoot.

In that moment, he becomes a new person. Let's not get too poetic about it, but he has lost a certain innocence. He must grapple with his role in a world that makes people shoot other people. He should have screamed when he had the chance.

Chances are, he'll play the tough guy. Now that he's no longer a
mere boy, he's expected to keep it all inside. This will haunt him.
It will give him nightmares a year later. You see, screaming is
normal; suppression is not. The agony of that grisly rite of passage will work its way out of him sooner or later. When he comes
home, he may need to talk about that experience, and he may
need a good cry.

The loss of innocence happens in other ways, too. Maybe it
was some sexual liaison on a R&R break. Maybe it was some bad
habits picked up from buddies. Hey, when you spend all week
bombing Iraqis, what's a little fun on the weekend? Who cares if
you start cursing or drinking or smoking? You're thousands of
miles from anyone who knows you, and there's a war on.

When such a person returns home, he's different from when he
left. He's older, more street smart, more cynical. He may have
more regrets. He has learned something about himself and become someone he's not sure he wants to be.

He, too, may need to talk about it. Or he may need to quietly
forgive himself. He may need to think about who he *does* want to
be, but he can never become the same person he was. The way
forward is not back.

Loss of Pride

Some players in the war effort also faced a loss of pride. This
war made some careers and broke others. It made Norman
Schwarzkopf. But if you're a rising peacetime officer and you go
over there and make some big errors in the crunch, that hurts you.
Some of the armed forces' press spokesmen became familiar
faces to us, but in the early going, some of them failed and were
replaced. They were giving out too much information or too
little, they were too uptight or too loose, until they found the right
guy. Careers were being shattered. These people had their shot at
bigtime success and did not succeed. But similar fortunes existed

up and down the ranks. The war brought great glory to some, but others had their shot at leadership, at heroism, at courage, and failed. They always thought they'd be ready when war came, but they weren't.

Such people return home to the fanfare but harbor a deep secret: They feel they don't deserve the acclaim. (One marine complained to me that he had received five medals for doing nothing but sitting on an assault ship and playing cards.) Many of them turn sour on their own abilities. Such humbling can be the start of a new outlook on life, if they pick themselves up and move on. They must accept themselves with all their faults and foibles and move on in directions in which they *can* succeed.

Personal Priorities

War can be addicting. Encamped on the edge of the action, you are regularly besieged by reporters and television crews. "What do you think? How do you feel? Anything to say to the folks back home?"

And the cameras are rolling again when the vets return home. "How does it feel? Great to be home, huh?" "Congratulations, you're a hero!"

The mass media savvy of this war made it fascinating for the viewers back home, but it may have tilted our whole perspective. The camera enlarges. Whatever the camera puts its lens on is news. It creates a significance that is larger than life. This magnification distorts the true picture of reality.

In the aftermath of the Delta crash, we found that a number of the nurses in the burn unit of the hospital were breaking down. These were crusty, experienced nurses who had seen it all. They had cared for patients far worse than the Delta victims. Our best explanation was that the media hype added pressure. Reporters were everywhere; reports were in the papers each day and on the news each night. That lent an extraordinary importance to these cases. The nurses were no longer just doing their jobs; the whole event had exploded into something far bigger than normal, and some of the nurses couldn't handle it.

Most of us divide our lives into sections. We work eight hours and go home to be with the family, maybe go out with friends. Each area of our lives is a department relatively free from the worries of other departments. When we begin to carry those worries around with us, we feel stressed.

Those nurses in Dallas had learned to compartmentalize. They had to. You care for people in the direst need for eight hours, but then you have to go home and enjoy life. The media hype, however, blew everything up so large that they couldn't compartmentalize. They'd go home after work, flip on the television, and watch a report on the crash burn victims. All their friends were asking about it. The nurses could no longer leave their work at the hospital, which created undue stress.

A similar phenomenon occurred in the gulf. Many soldiers had never done anything as significant as fight in this war. Hey, you're on television! You must be important! Every move you make is recorded for posterity. You're a hero; America salutes you. Out in the desert, there *are* no other compartments to your life, so you bask in the glory of the camera's eye. Naturally, you want to prolong that thrill as long as possible.

You come home to the flag waving and yellow ribbons. Your family is bursting with pride. Your town has a special rally to honor you. You're interviewed by that good-looking anchorperson. You speak at your kid's school.

But a month later, the cameras are gone. You're old news; someone else is returning from the gulf. Others are getting the red-carpet treatment. Your friends are beginning to yawn now as you tell the tale of the Scud alert.

Many people actually experience symptoms of withdrawal as the limelight fades. They're suffering from "glory addiction."

Everything else in their lives seems duller since the television lights aren't shining on it.

Others may get used to the excitement of being in war. It's terrifying to be in constant danger, but some learn to love that "on the edge" feeling. The adrenaline pumps, the heart beats faster, the eyes dart. Back home, everything is so drab. Some become "action junkies," always trying to replicate the excitement of their wartime experiences.

One man told me, "The thing I can't explain about Vietnam is how pleasurable it was." He went on to describe some horrible things he had done, killings and mutilations, but he added, "I can close my eyes and still feel the pleasure. How do I explain that something so horrible could be so pleasurable?"

I think it's just the high of the dangerous situation. His whole life was revved up at that point; every day was an adventure. When he came back and reprocessed the events, his mind quickly saw how horrific his actions were, but his body still remembered the rush he got back then. Fortunately, he was coming to grips with that. Some never do. They keep looking for that action high the rest of their lives.

Many vets came back from Vietnam and became emergency medical technicians. One chaplain I know was telling me about his post-Vietnam experiences as an EMT. On one occasion, he had rushed to a burning house, where some people needed emergency aid, and he flashed back to Vietnam. The flames, the cries, the urgency, the action were all the same. It suddenly clicked. He realized he was trying to replicate what he had felt in Vietnam. For him, that was destructive. He was burying himself in this job, working overtime, taking all the worst calls—all because he had never put Vietnam behind him.

Even those of us back home may acquire our own brand of action addiction. It was a major adjustment when CNN went back to its normal coverage of worldwide news. We were geared up for daily Scud reports, and now all we got was the latest word on the gross national product of Finland. The crisis mindset of those of us back home can create a rush that we may try to replicate, even after the vets are home.

Once again, the key word is *balance*. These addictions temporarily throw a person or family off balance. They twist priorities, shatter assumptions, make the real seem fake and the fake real. It may take some time to restore our sense of equilibrium, but that is what needs to happen.

10

Family Matters

"We're so used to seeing the movie version, when Joe gets off the carrier ship and embraces Mary and they walk off into the sunset and everything is happy ever after," says South Carolina psychology professor Thomas Cafferty. "Studies from World War II and Vietnam have tended to show reunions are very difficult and stressful."[1]

"People think we're going to have three days of satin sheets and all will be wonderful," says Tucson psychologist Dennis Embry, who writes booklets on readjustment for military families. "Evidence shows that this is the most difficult time of all."[2]

Army chaplain Chet Lanious gave redeployment briefings to returning troops before they left Saudi Arabia. The talk went something like this:

> Some of you guys are going to get back to base, your wife is going to drive you home, fix you a nice meal, and tell you over the main course she wants a divorce. Or some of you may find your wife is four months pregnant and you've been

over here for seven months. Or everything you own is in a
pawnshop and your car has been repossessed.[3]

Early reports indicate that Lanious's predictions are coming
true. One lawyer near Fort Bragg, North Carolina, has handled
three times her normal load of divorce cases since the troops
began returning home.[4]

War hurts people. War also hurts families. Let's take a look at
some of these problems and see what can be done about them.

Infidelity

We live in a sex-crazy age. "How can a person possibly get
along without sex for six, seven months?" The spirit of celibacy
is not raging in America today.

Obviously, infidelity happens on both sides of the ocean. Even
though opportunities for sexual liaisons in the gulf were somewhat limited by Muslim restrictions, still there were R&R
leaves—not to mention male and female personnel working
closely together. This creates new problems. It's not just "a girl
in every port," but "a girl in my unit who is coming back to the
States, too." There is a greater chance that flings will turn into
full-fledged affairs that threaten marriages.

The spouses at home may have been trying to fill needs that
were more than sexual. Loneliness was common. Some who
were suddenly in the position of single parents needed help with
the kids. (A child-care worker near Fort Bragg tells of numerous
"uncles" who began picking up the children.)[5]

This does not excuse marital infidelity, but it may help us
understand it. War is crazy. It makes people do crazy things. The
added stress of wartime—on both those in the gulf and those at
home—pushed many to do uncharacteristic things.

How should you deal with this situation?

Look forward, not backward Don't dwell on the hurt, the

betrayal, the absence, or even your own guilt. Look ahead to the kind of relationship you want. How will you strengthen your marriage against future temptations?

Now is the time to recommit yourself to the future of your marriage.

Be honest but not hurtful As you look forward and plan your marriage's future strength, you may realize that it isn't strong enough *right now* to handle your admission of infidelity. Your goal should be to get to a point where you can be totally open and forgiving about this.

Forgive and be forgiven If the infidelity is out on the table, accept it and forgive it. If you are the guilty party, accept your guilt and your partner's forgiveness.

"Distance"

The returning partner may clam up. The homebound spouse is dying for information. He or she wants to share in the whole experience. But the returning spouse (and face it, this is usually a male thing) keeps it all inside.

Why? Maybe it wasn't all it was cracked up to be. Maybe the person doesn't want to relive it. Maybe he's trying to compartmentalize his experience—gulf and wife don't belong in the same sentence. Maybe he doesn't know what to say.

In many homes, the wife nags, the husband keeps quiet. "I want to be a part of this experience!" the wife is saying underneath it all. *Leave me alone,* the husband is thinking. *I can handle this myself!*

What's the answer? Try some of these.

Keep a journal The returning spouse should keep a private journal to record thoughts and memories. Don't worry about complete sentences and proper grammar; just write your thoughts as they come. Describe the experience of camping in the desert.

What was it like to prepare for war? Who were the others in your unit? What were they like? How did you feel on January 16–17, on February 23–24?

You don't need to share this with anyone until you're good and ready, but it may be easier to show this journal to your spouse than to talk about your experiences.

Get together with army buddies If you find yourself not talking about the war with your spouse, it may be that you're still processing some of your feelings and think your spouse won't understand. It may help to find others who have been in the gulf and share your feelings with them.

Be patient The spouse at home can gently nudge but shouldn't shove. The time will come when the returning spouse feels secure enough to open up about the war experience. Do not personalize his refusal to do so. It is not a reflection on you (that is, it does not mean you aren't sensitive or caring enough). He's just trying to find his own equilibrium right now.

Changes in Spouse

One of the biggest changes returning husbands will see is in wives who have been forced to fend for themselves. They have gained a certain amount of independence that may be hard for the returning husband to accept.

Other changes may occur, as well. The shock of war may have made the returning spouse more sober, more anxious, or more thirsty for alcohol. The months of waiting may have made the spouse at home patient or impatient, caring or uncaring. Whatever the changes, one thing is certain: After that long a time apart, you will not be reunited with the same person you left. Both partners will have changed.

Remember: People are always changing. We're used to changing together. We see changes in each other at incremental stages, and we get used to them bit by bit. Seven months of changes may be tough to take all at once. But you can't go back. Accept the new person your spouse is, celebrate the changes, and move on from there.

Take time out. Try a second honeymoon to get to know each other again.

Communicate. Talk about your changes. Answer these questions together:

How do you think you have changed?

How do I think you have changed?

How do you think I have changed?

How do I think I have changed?

What do I like about the way you've changed?

What do I dislike about the way you've changed?

What do you like about the way I've changed?

What do you dislike about the way I've changed?

How should we both change from here?

What can we do, beginning this week, to make that happen?

Lost Time With Family

Birthdays, graduations, first steps, first words, first communion, first date, Little League games, school plays; the events of a child's life can come fast and furious. Leave for seven months and you miss a ton of them.

This can create resentment in some children. They know their mother or father is just doing his or her job. But they feel deprived and they're not sure whom to blame.

Those special moments are lost forever to the absent parent. You can mourn for them as you would mourn any loss. You can try to reclaim some of them, but this isn't always possible. You must, however, restore relationships with all your children and move on from there.

In some cases, a child will "turn bad" when a parent is away. The family's discipline structure breaks down, and the kid gets away with murder. Resentment can turn to bitterness and rejection, and the child may stop communicating, even when the absent parent returns. This may be an attempt to "punish" the parent for going away.

Many families struggle with such problems, and there are no easy answers. But here are some some thoughts for families of gulf returnees:

Make sure the children know what you were doing and why You may assume that the kids know what it means to "serve your country." They may not.

Admit your pain   Did it hurt you to be away from your family? Then admit that to your kids. Sometimes vets (especially men) try hard to be tough, resistant, just-doing-my-job. But your children need to see how much you ached to be with them.

Keep a family journal   Encourage all the kids to write down or draw pictures of their experiences, thoughts, and feelings in the time the military parent was away. Collect these entries over the next year and go through it at the one-year anniversary of the return.

For kids who may be finding it hard to communicate, encourage them to start journaling their feelings. You must assure them of their privacy. Promise that you will not read their journals unless they ask you to.

Family roundtable   Start a tradition at dinner or some other time in which one family member (a different one each time) gets to ask one question of the returning parent, and the parent asks one question in return. The questions should refer to events or feelings during the war. This may keep the whole family from being overwhelmed with catch-up information.

Date your kids   Make a special "date" with each of your children individually, and catch up on all that happened while you were away.

Changes in Family Systems

In the middle of this basketball season, Charles Barkley, the star forward for the Philadelphia 76ers, was out with an injury for a couple of weeks. The team had to learn to function without him. The first few games were rough, but then other players stepped in to fill Barkley's roles, and the team was running smoothly once again. Then Barkley returned. If they were that good without him, they would be awesome with him back in the lineup, right? Wrong. They were blown out in his first game back. It was another game or two before they learned how to play with him again.

That can happen in families, too. A parent leaves, and it's a shock. But the family learns to function. The other spouse takes on new duties, and the kids pitch in. Soon they're a smoothly running machine again. Then the parent comes back from the war and has to fit in again. It's not easy.

Be flexible   Accept the fact that some family members have learned their new roles well. If Junior is used to taking out the trash, let him.

Leave room for others to use their skills   One veteran marine's wife has learned to leave certain repairs undone, so he can do them when he gets back, "so he feels needed, like he's the man of the house." She says she knows how to do almost everything herself by now, but "sometimes you've done it so long, you go ahead and don't involve him when he comes back, which can cause problems."[6]

The returning spouse must be aware of this, too. I talked to one man whose wife had handled the finances while he was away. "My checkbook had never been in such great shape," he says. She's still paying the bills now, even after his return.

Communicate Talk with your spouse and with your kids. Discuss the idea of the family as a machine, as a system in which all parts should be happy and doing what they do best. Discuss how the "parts" could be happier and how the whole family could function best. This sort of communication and group planning can do a great deal to restore children's and spouses' sense of control and contribution to the family.

The Gulf War was an earthquake, shifting the foundations of many families. The aftershocks will continue to be felt for months and years afterward. But families that develop good habits of communication and flexibility will stand strong amid these tremors.

11

Economic Sanctions

Cut off their ability to trade with the outside world. That will weaken their economy. Then all their attention and resources are focused on preparation for war. This further destabilizes their economic standing.

The strategy seemed to work against Saddam Hussein, whose country is economically devastated.

It also seemed to work against the families of many United States troops.

Pay Cuts

Yes, we do pay our soldiers, but for many in reserve or National Guard units, military pay is a fraction of what they make in their normal jobs. In all, 227,400 reservists and National Guardsmen were activated (though only 80,000 of these served in the gulf).[1] If even half of these had to take pay cuts to serve in the war, that's a lot of families operating under budget for half a year or more.

What happens when one of these soldiers returns from duty?
The war is just beginning. Credit cards are maxxed out. The bills
are overdue. The bank is threatening to foreclose. The kids need
new sneakers. The way most Americans live, close to the edge of
their budgets, this could put many families in a hole for years to
come.

Yellow Ribbons, Pink Slips

In August 1990, the United States economy was in sad shape.
We were actually beginning to hear the word *recession*. In the
months that followed, the national economy continued to be sluggish. This meant layoffs and unemployment.

Look at the bright side. The people in our armed forces were
employed. They didn't have to go through all those layoffs—until
their return. Many had no jobs to return to. There is a federal law
protecting the jobs of returning vets, but there are loopholes. If an
employer can establish that the vet would have been laid off if he
or she had remained on the job, the vet does not have to be
rehired. In sluggish times, that's not hard to establish.

The employer is not necessarily a villain in this, either. Recession forces companies into life-or-death decisions, too. One
salary, or one job left undone, can mean the difference between
success or failure. Still, it's no fun for the vet to come home from
sitting in the sand and waiting, only to sit in his living room
reading the want ads.

Or think of the many self-employed people who served, or
those in very small businesses. What will their business be like
on their return? One reservist lawyer tells of referring his clients
to other lawyers before he left. How many of those will he get
back?[2] It may take a while to rebuild the business.

Loss of Seniority, Promotion

After the welcome-home party, you learn that your former
office mate is now a vice president. That's the job you were
gunning for.

There's a new computer-training course at work that you missed getting into. You'll have to wait for next year.

Or you return to college as a junior when all your friends are seniors. You lost a year, and your readjustment pressures may hurt your class standing.

The Supreme Court has ruled that a returning veteran should not lose seniority but get the same credit he would have if he had stayed at his job. And it should be said that there is, generally, great support for returning vets.

Still, a job opens and you're out in the desert somewhere. Someone else is going to fill it. In a million unofficial ways, opportunities come up that the vet misses out on. These can often circumvent the court's ruling.

A case came up in Seattle where a hospital pharmacist serving in the gulf came back to find that someone else had taken his boss's place. He felt that he deserved that job and would have gotten it had he stayed home.[3]

Diminished Ability

What if you find it harder to concentrate at your old job? You keep flashing back to Saudi. The lunch whistle sounds like a Scud alert and sets you on edge all afternoon. Nightmares rob you of sleep, and the resulting lethargy makes you inefficient on the job.

Even the most gracious employer may find it hard to keep you. "Hey, we appreciate you serving your country and all, but we have to get some work out of you." This may be the unkindest cutback of all—not a layoff but a firing, because you can't do the job anymore.

In some cases, spouses and parents of those in the gulf experienced this kind of diminished ability. Their preoccupation with the war kept them from concentrating on their work. Smart employers provided counseling and support groups for such employees. Still, some spouses may have added to the family's financial woes by working less efficiently during the conflict.

Bungled Finances

You may return to find that your spouse (or whoever you left with your checkbook) has strafed your accounts. The numbers don't add up. The account is overdrawn. You have twenty-three magazines coming to your home because he or she can't say no to telephone solicitors. The overzealous mechanic talked your spouse into an overhaul of the engine when it just needed a new muffler. All your kids now have braces. And for some reason you can't figure out, there's new vinyl siding on the house. Then there's that big guy, Bruno, who keeps showing up to collect car payments.

It happens. Sure, some vets returned to find their finances in impeccable order, but others encountered this kind of chaos, and a few have found that their unscrupulous mates or lovers have robbed them blind. She's living in the Caribbean somewhere, and there's a convenience store where your house used to be.

What to Do?

How do you start to pick up the pieces?

Don't let money problems destroy your relationships As you know, finances are a leading cause of divorce. Don't look for someone to blame. Accept the situation and work together to solve the problems.

Seek financial help soon There is still a good feeling about the war. People feel gratitude to the returning vets. Take advantage of that. Don't try to make it on your own if you're in a deep financial crisis. Talk to a banker and negotiate a reasonable loan. Call your creditors and arrange payment plans. Believe it or not,

once you get past the computers, there are usually people who
will understand your plight.

Use the help the military provides   There are agencies to help
you deal with situations of financial need. Don't be too proud to
use these. They're there for you. (*See* Resources.)

Don't be overwhelmed   The onslaught of economic problems
can keep you from dealing with any of them. Take them one by
one. Take a long-range view of your road back to financial health.
It's the same with a job search: Set your goals day by day, week
by week.

Don't battle your employer (unless you really have to)   If
you've been laid off, passed over, demoted, or fired for postwar
inefficiency, try to communicate with your employer as best you
can. You may be able to work together to find a solution that
works for both of you. Chances are, your employer doesn't want
to be a "bad guy." Treating a gulf vet unfairly is not good PR,
inside or outside the company.

But look at it from your employer's perspective as well. If you
are less productive because of postwar stress, it hurts your company. Perhaps you can work out a temporary part-time or limited-
expectation arrangement until you're back to full stride.

Know your rights and use them   The Labor Department uses
the "escalator principle" in talking about the level at which a vet
should be rehired. Each company has an escalator, of sorts, on
which people's careers go up (and in some cases, down). You
may leave to serve in a war, but the escalator keeps going up.
Where would you be if you had stayed? That's the operative
question. If you have a complaint about the level at which you've
been rehired (or if you haven't been rehired), you can call your
local Veterans Employment and Training Service (VETS), an

agency of the Labor Department. They will seek to negotiate a
solution for you, and if that doesn't work, you may take it to
court.

Keep your self-esteem   Easier said than done, right? I know
this sounds like psychobabble, but it's a crucial issue related to
economics. For some reason, many of us (especially men) attach
a great deal of our self-worth to our finances. If we're poor, we
feel worthless. (Ironically, we talk about our personal "net
worth." Believe me, your net worth is far more than your bank
account.)

Don't buy into that lie. You have served your country. You
can be proud of that. If you find yourself in financial straits, that's
a sacrifice you have made. Get the help that's coming to you, but
if you're still in economic trouble, you can bear that burden with
pride. Slowly, surely, you can make it back to solvency. But you
can feel good about yourself each step of the way.

Part III

Healing the Wounds of War

12

The Next Stage Leaves in Ten Minutes

When Delta Flight 191 crashed at the Dallas–Fort Worth Airport on August 2, 1985, I rushed into action. As a chaplain in the local Air National Guard Unit, I was assigned to coordinate all ministry functions to the families of crash victims. One hundred thirty-seven people died in that disaster.

The families converged on the Airport Hilton. Some didn't believe their loved ones had died; they wanted to go out to the crash site and search. Others seemed convinced that their friends had been on another flight. They dealt with their grief by denying it.

Various emotional releases were evident. One man walked around in front of the hotel in tears. Sobbing, he told me he had lost his "baby daughter." Many were angry at Delta, at God, even at me! Someone had to be blamed.

"What did you tell people?" That's something I am often asked. But the very question fascinates and bothers me. Why do we assume that we must have the right answers for people in trauma? Do we imagine that the "magic words" will make the problems go away?

In the Jewish culture, there are several wise traditions that accompany the grieving process. One is the *shiva,* in which mourners come for two or three evenings to "sit with" the bereaved family. That's what the Hebrew word *shiva* means, to sit. In its simplicity, that tradition embodies some great truths. First, healing happens best in community. Second, the best thing we can do for grievers is to be there for them.

There are no magic words.

I have discovered that the best way to help is to be a mourning partner. Chaplain Robert Parlotz defines a mourning partner like this: "A person who stands with an individual while s/he works through grief, anticipatory grief, and bereavement . . . the mourning partner, thus, is a helper, an enabler, and therefore is a provider of support and suggester of appropriate action."[1]

In the aftermath of the Gulf War, there are different kinds of grieving. Some are, in fact, mourning the deaths of loved ones. Some returnees have serious physical injuries. But for many, many others, the loss was more emotional than physical.

We must not make light of the grieving process by diluting it too much, because even minor losses can become major problems if not dealt with properly. It will help if we learn to grieve properly for them.

Stages of Grief

There's a second Jewish tradition that can teach us: the "unveiling." Six months to a year after a husband's death, there is a small ceremony in which the widow removes her veil of mourning. The act symbolizes the end of her grieving process; it is time to get on with life.

This teaches us two key things: The grieving process will

eventually end as the mourner accepts the death and reenters life, but it takes some time to get there.

In the quote above, Parlotz speaks of people working through grief. There's a process involved. It takes time and some emotional effort.

Elisabeth Kübler-Ross has written several books on stages of grief, but she is just one of many scholars in the field. Various writers have observed five or six emotional stages that people go through in coming to terms with a loved one's death or their own terminal illness.

In Kübler-Ross's paradigm, these stages (or coping mechanisms) are:

• Denial
• Anger
• Bargaining
• Depression
• Acceptance

Most postwar trauma reactions follow a similar pattern, evolving from one stage to another.

We must remember that this is a *healthy* progression. Those grieving any type of loss are not wrong to be in denial or to feel anger or to attempt bargaining. This is a process that must be worked *through*.

Problems arise when we get stuck at one stage or another. The widow who still sets a place at dinner for her husband after three years is stuck in denial. She needs to move on. Yet that would be very normal behavior in the first six months or so after a spouse's death.

It might help to look at the theories of Carl A. Nighswonger. He presents six "dramas" that a trauma recoverer goes through, each of which has a healthy response and an unhealthy response.

The healthy responses correspond somewhat to Kübler-Ross's five stages.

Drama	Healthy Response	Unhealthy Response
Shock	Denial	Panic
Emotion	Anger/Catharsis	Depression/Guilt/Shame
Negotiation	Bargaining	Selling Out/Withdrawal
Cognition	Hope/Search for	Bitterness/Despair/
	Meaning	Gloom
Commitment	Acceptance	Resignation
Completion	Fulfillment	Forlornness

In each drama of the trauma sufferer's life, he or she has a choice: Move ahead in a healthy way or settle it. Notice that each of the unhealthy responses is a backward step. The healthy responses keep us moving forward. Denial eventually breaks on the shoals of reality, unless panic keeps us from facing reality. Anger plays itself out, unless we turn it in toward ourselves.

The problem with these charts, however, is that they're too simple. Yes, there may be a general forward movement through these stages, but people slip back all the time. In a way it's like a video game in which you play through the first screen to get to the second and third, but if you fail at the third, you start over. People may bounce from depression to bargaining with God to anger, back to original denial, and ultimately to acceptance.

Charles R. Figley, a leading authority on stress reactions among Vietnam vets, helps us see the cyclical nature of recovery. He lists the stages of recovery as follows:

    I. catastrophe
   II. relief and confusion
  III. avoidance
  IV. reconsideration
   V. adjustment

While there is a steady progression from I to V, there is still a fair amount of slippage. Figley shows us a combination of dealing and not dealing with the issues. Part of stage II ("relief and confusion") is the question of "How much do I need to emotionally process this catastrophe?" As we begin to process it—to come to terms with the horror, fear, grief, and so forth—we inevitably have more than we can handle. So we enter into stage III (avoidance). When it's safe enough to reenter the waters of processing, we move again—usually forward to the mental reconsideration of stage IV, but sometimes there are some emotions that need reprocessing, so we go back.

I like to interpret this as a three-level process of coping with a trauma: emotional, behavioral, and mental.

Initial Shock
Numbness
Denial
Fantasy
Hysteria

Emotional Releases
Anger
Depression
Crying
Praying/Bargaining with God

Behavioral Processes
Going back to work
Resuming other life-style actions
Discarding relics of what or who was lost
Commitment to meaningful activities and relationships

Mental Acceptance
Why did this happen?
How did it happen?
How have I changed?
How do I need to change?

There should be a general progression through these stages. There is a gradual maturing, a coming to grips with the situation. It must be repeated that this process is a healthy one. It is not wrong to be at an early point, for instance, dealing with the emotional releases. It takes some people longer than others to get through the various stages. We must not force the issue.

13

Healing the Hurts

Once upon a time, there was a man who set out on a journey to the Great North. He had friends who had moved there, and their postcards said it was lovely.

As he traveled, he had to pass through the Wild Woods. He had heard stories of the creatures that lurked there, mauling an occasional passerby. Yet he fancied himself a strong warrior and swift of foot (in case he had to flee).

He had scarcely set foot in the Wild Woods when a huge lion attacked him. He managed to return a few blows, but he received some painful wounds as well. It was all he could do to get out of the lion's grip and race northward.

In a few minutes, with the lion at his heels, he encountered a giant bear, which swiped at him, knocking him off the road. He scrambled to his feet in time to escape again. Soon a gorilla and tiger joined the chase, each licking its lips in anticipation of its tasty prey.

He was indeed swift of foot, and by nightfall he noticed that the growls had faded behind him. He was safe for the moment, safe enough to wall himself in.

As luck would have it, he came upon an old rock slide. With considerable effort, he piled up rocks, patching them with mud from a nearby stream, shoring them up with timber from the woods. By midnight, he had built four strong walls around himself. Those beasts would never get him now. He nursed his wounds and slept.

When morning came—it must have been morning, though he couldn't see the sun—he heard the growls of those beasts once again. They were pounding against his southern wall. He prided himself on the strength of his construction, until the bear's paw knocked a stone loose and shot through the opening. He beat at the paw with a club and it withdrew. But before he could patch the hole in his wall, the lion's paw came through, narrowly missing him. It was a scary existence for several hours, as he dodged the paws that intruded into his little fort.

Then he heard voices, human voices, from the north. "Can we help?" they were calling.

"I don't know," he called out. "I'm trapped."

Then he heard his name. He recognized the voice of an old friend who had moved north years ago. "Is that you?" the voice asked.

Through his tears, the man said, "Yes."

"Listen carefully," his friend said. "You have to take down the wall."

"Are you crazy?" the man yelled. "There are man-eating beasts out there!"

"We know," another voice assured. "But we can't help you unless you let us in. Just take down your northern wall," his friend added. "Then we'll help you tame those beasts."

"Tame those beasts?" the traveler screamed. "You don't know how vicious they are. If I take down the wall, they will come around and eat me. They'll get you, too!"

"No," said the other voice sternly. "We have learned the secret of taming the beasts. But your walls here are blocking the road. We cannot tame them unless you let us in."

The man refused for several days. Every day, the people from the north came and begged him to let them help. Every day, he was too afraid.

But finally he had grown weary of dodging the intruding paws. His wounds were not healing. He needed medical attention, and they had good doctors in the Great North. Slowly, carefully, he began to dismantle his northern wall.

Once he began, the people were there to help take down the stones. After one large stone was removed, his old friend crawled in and embraced him.

When the last stones of the northern and side walls were taken down, the leader of this group turned to the traveler and said, "Shall we take down the southern wall now?"

He was filled with new fear. "But the beasts are out there!"

"We will tame them," he said. "Trust us."

"But you haven't seen them!" he sobbed. "They are huge! You don't know how ferocious they are!"

"We do," the man's friend said, patting his arm. "We have tamed others."

Just then, the tiger's paw shot through the opening in the southern wall. One of the helpers brandished a saltshaker and managed a few shakes before the tiger withdrew.

"What was that?" the man asked, bewildered.

The leader responded calmly, "Salt. The tiger will lick it off, then get thirsty, then go down to the stream and drink."

"And then he'll be gone?"

"Oh, no," the leader smiled. "They always come back. But after three or four trips to the stream, they seem happy, docile. They don't want to eat you anymore."

"And that really works?" the man asked his friend.

"Usually. Nine times out of ten."

"And the tenth time?"

"Well," the friend smiled, "that's why we're all wearing track shoes."

The leader turned to the traveler again. "What do you say? Can we take down this wall?"

Reluctantly, the man said, "I guess so."

"*You* have to take down the first stone."

That was even harder to do. But, supported by his friend, he removed the topmost stone on the wall. Then the other helpers joined in, taking down a few more stones.

"Stop!" called the leader.

"Why are we stopping?" the traveler said. "I thought we were supposed to take down this wall."

"We want to deal with the animals one at a time," his friend explained, "so we have to keep part of the wall up."

Sure enough, the gorilla—the tallest of the creatures—reached over the wall. A quick-moving helper sprinkled him with salt.

"He's going away," said another, peering through a crack in the wall.

"All right," the leader ordered, "let's take down a few more stones." In this slow, halting manner, the wall came down. At one point, they actually had to put some stones back up, but the danger passed. The salt treatment seemed to work. Within hours, the animals were sated, lying quietly by the roadside. Some of the helpers were even petting them. They invited the traveler to pet the beasts, too, but he couldn't do it.

By nightfall they were all on their way again, headed for the Great North.

This story illustrates the situation of many war veterans. They have had to pass through the Wild Woods of war. In order to survive, they have put up walls. This is not some personality disorder—it is a survival tactic. You simply cannot deal with the ferocious facts of war all at once. You must wall yourself off in self-defense.

Unfortunately, like the traveler in the story, some build too many walls and keep them up longer than they need to. Walls may separate them from the people who love them, those who can help them. It is a scary thing to take down those walls, but through love and trust, it must be done.

Researchers have drawn a parallel between emotional trauma reactions and the human body's physical reaction to a foreign element within it. Whether it is some object piercing the skin or some diseased tissue, our bodies take steps to wall off the troubled area. After the initial trauma, the wounded area may go numb. This is a defense mechanism that allows us to survive as the healing process begins to take place.

It is the same way with emotional trauma. Our minds often "wall off" the troubled area. On the battlefield, in the heat of doing the job, the terror gets put aside. But later, the memories come back. Healing still has to take place. It's only natural.

The feeling doesn't return to a wounded area all at once. As our bodies heal, the feeling returns. Slowly, the walls come down. And that can hurt! We can wish for the return of numbness, but the body continues to deal with the wound by healing and restoring feeling.

So it is during the recovery period for emotional trauma. The symptoms include both a continued numbing effect and the painful return of feeling. It's as if our minds are regulating how much we can deal with at each step along the way.

Let's look back over those symptoms of stress reactions to see how our minds dismantle those walls. We'll use the criteria that the American Psychiatric Association has set up for recognizing post-traumatic stress disorder:

> 1. Existence of a recognizable stressor that would evoke significant symptoms of distress in almost anyone. [The war in the gulf certainly qualifies.]

2. Reexperiencing the trauma, as evidenced by at least
one of the following:
  recurrent and intrusive recollections of the event;
  recurrent dreams of the event;
  sudden acting or feeling as if the traumatic event were
     reoccurring.
[Flashbacks in various forms bring back to our minds the
issues that must be dealt with.]
3. Numbing of responsiveness to [the external world] or
reduced involvement with the external world, as shown by
one or more of the following:
  markedly diminished interest in one or more significant
     activities;
  feelings of detachment or estrangement from others;
  constricted affect [that is, a lack of display of emotion].
  [So here the numbness remains. It's a defense mechanism. The walls are still up.]
4. At least two of the following symptoms that were not
present before the trauma:
  hyperalertness or exaggerated startle response;
  sleep disturbance;
  guilt about surviving when others have not;
  memory impairment or trouble concentrating;
  avoidance of activities that arouse recollection of the trau-
     matic events;
  intensification of symptoms by exposure to events that
     symbolize or resemble the traumatic event
  [various ways of dealing with and nondealing with the
catastrophe].

Many of these symptoms occur in the natural working out of a
trauma. It's all part of taking down the walls slowly, bit by bit.
Troubles occur when:

• A person never takes down the walls.
• A person takes down the wrong wall, removing the

"southern" wall and attempting to defeat the beasts on his own, rather than taking down the "northern" wall and letting his friends help.

• Dismantling the wall too quickly, so that the beasts (memories of catastrophe) scare him into putting it up again.

In any of these scenarios, a person can get stuck on the way to the final stage of acceptance.

How Can We Help?

What if you're one of these friends? How can you help tame the beasts? How can you help bring down those walls?

The hardest thing for many would-be helpers to understand is that *the wounded person has to take down the first stone from the wall.* You can't force this. You can encourage, support, console, be there, but you mustn't rush things.

Remember that in situations of deep grief, the ideal comforter is a mourning partner. A support person can accompany a wounded person through the stages of recovery, but each person must take his own steps.

The best you can do is to show the way out. Often a recovering person feels trapped in a certain stage. As a comforter, you can offer a way of escape. This keeps the person moving forward, not backward, through the recovery process.

14

Regaining Control

Bruce Lundgren, one of the hostages held by the militants in Iran in the late 1970s, has said, "We're like tea bags. We don't know our strength until we get into hot water."

That is the case with many of us. As long as life is easy, we never have to call up our reserves of strength. But that strength is there, waiting to be mobilized. When we encounter a situation of grief or loss or great stress, we can summon those reserves. Dr. Julius Segal writes, "Indeed, until recently, the human capacity for conquering life's crises appears to have been one of psychology's best-kept secrets."[1]

So far, this book has discussed the many problems that arise as a result of war, especially as a result of this Gulf War. The problems have been emphasized because there is a popular image of this war as problem-free. We swept in there, bombed the Iraqis, and came home, right? Well, in many ways, we bombed ourselves, too, although the devastation may not be apparent.

I want sufferers to know that they're not alone and they won't be forgotten. I also want them to know that healing will happen. You may have taken a pounding—emotionally, economically, relationally—but there is strength in you and around you that will help you rebuild.

I remember being with a couple whose child was brain dead. I was sitting there with the couple while their physician, a leading expert in the field, was going around and around and around, trying to explain that there was no hope for the child's recovery. In this very intense situation, the mother looked at the doctor and said, "This is very difficult for you, isn't it?"

I looked at this woman and wondered, *Where in the world did that come from?* In the context of one of the most painful experiences imaginable, the loss of her daughter, she looked out and realized that this doctor was having a rough time. In a way it was her human touch that liberated *him.*

God has put in each one of us the ability to bounce back, to cope, to come back to wholeness after devastating experiences. How does this occur? How can we help the process happen?

Communicate

First, talk about what you've been through. I have already mentioned the need to take down your walls. Open up your broken heart, clear the pipeline of feelings, give your sorrow words.

In *Macbeth,* Shakespeare wrote, "Give sorrow words. The grief that does not speak whispers in the overwrought heart and bids it break." Until we articulate what we are feeling, we cannot begin to heal. Researchers see a vital link between the strength of a person's social supports and his own resilience in times of stress. The more a person can talk with his friends about his trying experiences, the stronger he will be in coping with them. This says a lot about the value of friends and small groups and basic human touch.

Why is this? Why is it so important to talk about things? Let me suggest four reasons:

Putting feelings into words helps us overcome our fears of being seen as weak and unworthy This especially applies to men. We males, our culture says, are not supposed to be weak or cry.

We have learned this from Rambo and John Wayne and a host of earlier role models. I remember once as a boy when I was fishing with my grandfather. Hooking a worm, I stuck my finger instead. As I begin to sniffle, you know what my grandfather said to me? "Men don't cry."

But we do! It's the most natural thing in the world. We have just learned to keep our feelings inside, where those fears and feelings fester.

Articulating our experience enables us to communicate with others who have been through the same things Others have dealt with similar hardships *and survived*. So can we. That mutuality can give us great strength to cope with our situations.

A friend of mine, Gary, was a POW in Vietnam for seven years. For four of those years, he was kept in a small box, four feet by four feet, in total darkness. How did he survive?

He says that every so often he would hear, from the darkness outside the box, the voice of another prisoner saying, "Gary, have a nice day." He could live another month on those words. His friend had risked his life to say those few words. That little shred of communication meant everything.

It helps us to see that our feelings are not abnormal but normal Chances are, when you start to talk about your feelings, you'll say something like, "This is really nothing, but . . ." or "This may sound strange, but. . . ." The fact is, it's probably not strange at all. Abnormal circumstances bring forth unusual responses. That's to be expected. In wartime, the book of what's "normal" gets totally rewritten.

It helps us find our first practical steps in dealing with our losses When you start talking, you start doing. You can talk with friends about what job you're going to get or what doctor you're going to see or when you're planning to have a reunion of your unit. Talking is the spark that makes things happen.

Get Control

A second way of coping with loss is to regain some control over our lives. You've lived for the better part of a year at the whim of the United States government. The service says, "Jump!" And you say, "Where?" They say, "Dhahran," or "Kuwait City," or "Fort Bragg." Or they say, "Don't jump just yet, but be ready to jump at any moment."

I'm making light of a tough situation. (Joking about things is one way to regain control.) If you experienced a major loss— injury, family problems, death of a friend—it may be especially bothersome that this terrible thing happened *and you had no control over it*. Your life has been radically changed, and you had no say in it.

One common reaction (an unhealthy one) is to give up all control, to let the forces of the government, of your family, of your job, just sweep you along. Often a grieving spouse will "let himself go." He or she will stop caring about his or her own appearance or health or relationships. What does it matter?

The road to wholeness involves regaining control of your life. One man told me that he had stopped shaving after his wife's death. He regained control by starting that ritual again each morning. For another man, it was jogging. "If I can do that one thing every day," he said, "I'll start to regain control of my life." One family I know put together a photo album after the father had died. They cried their way through the whole experience, but it was a healthy way of *doing something* with their grief.

If nothing else, I'd suggest that you begin keeping a journal. Go to a convenience store and pick up a cheap notebook and decide that you will fill a page a day with your thoughts. This will help you begin to regain control, and it may help prompt some communication, if you find that difficult.

General Dozier was held hostage by the Red Army in Italy back in the 1980s. I gave the invocation once at a banquet in his honor. He says that he kept control during his captivity by doing push-ups every morning. That simple act helped maintain his sanity.

He also experienced regular sessions in which his captors would try to indoctrinate him with Communist theory. In his own mind, he began to mull over everything he knew about communism, thinking up questions to ask, challenges to make, and so forth. He began to view it as a time when he could learn from them about what they believed. In essence, it was like a college class. He would "study up" in his mind for the one hour each day when he could discuss politics with them. He began to look forward to those times, because he was in control. He gained mental stimulation from their "indoctrination" sessions.

I don't know what it may be for you: push-ups, volunteer work, getting a college degree. But take control of your life. It will help you toward wholeness.

And *don't rush this process*. It takes different people different amounts of time to regain control of their lives. I have often thought that our culture doesn't deal with death and grief very well. Our funeral processes take a few days at most, then we're expected to be normal again.

In other cultures, it often takes six months to a year of remembering the deceased person in various ways before the grieving process is officially completed. They realize that it takes time to regain control and get back to normal.

The same could be said for any situation of loss. Whatever you lost out there in the desert, it may take some time to get over it. Start the process, but don't hurry it, and don't let others hurry you, either.

So what happens a year from now, when you seem to be doing okay again? Let's say you experienced a substantial loss. A buddy was killed in Desert Storm, or you and your wife broke up in the aftermath, or you missed all your kids' birthdays and they were mad at you for months. Anyhow, it's a year from now, you're getting back to normal, and you go the beach.

Sand.

Lots of it.

It all comes back to you. You feel tremendous remorse over your friend, your marriage, or the lost birthdays. What's wrong? Is this a relapse? Do you have to start over?

No. You have experienced a loss, and that loss will always be there. You will always feel bad about it. But it doesn't have to control your life. That's what wholeness is about. *Accept the loss, but cope with the pain.* The memories will come back five, ten years from now. That's fine. You may cry a little. But you have taken control of your life. That is as whole as you need to be.

Helping Others

I want to shift gears for a moment and speak directly to the friends and loved ones of returning vets. How can you specifically help them through this healing process?

Charles R. Figley, the post-traumatic stress expert, writes of a study that sought to discover *what kind of help was most helpful* to people undergoing stress. The researchers found five areas of crucial aid:

1. Emotional Support. "How are you feeling? That's okay. We're on your side."

2. Encouragement. "You're important to us." "You can
get over this." "You went through a lot, and you're
coping with it well, considering."
3. Advice. "Maybe you should see this doctor." "Here's
where you could get a loan." "Maybe you and your wife
should get away for a while."
4. Companionship. "Let's go to a ball game." "You
wanna come over and just hang out?" "I'm going shopping, want to join me?"
5. Tangible Aid. "Here's some money to tide you over.
You can pay me back later." "Why don't I take the kids
while you and hubby go off somewhere." "Sure, I'll
drive you to the clinic."[2]

In addition to these practical issues, here are some more the-
oretical strategies to consider.

Grant permission to grieve   Researchers have found that there
is a "hierarchy" to grief, especially in military situations. If a
commanding officer openly shows his feelings of sorrow over
some loss, then those in his command will be freer to do so. But
if an officer maintains a stone countenance, the troops will tend
to bottle up their feelings. In a way, the commander has to grant
"permission" to grieve.

That may occur in a family unit as well, or in other social
situations (especially among men). A man may feel that he has to
hold back his feeling to play the role of The Strong Man of the
House. Other family members and friends can do him a great
favor by encouraging open displays of sorrow or concern.

Help the vet recast his assumptions   I've talked about that
"circle of assumptions." Part of the recovery process is a matter
of enlarging those circles to embrace some of the events we don't
understand. A person may need help in doing that. Talk about the

meaning of what happened, but don't be afraid to admit what you can't figure out.

Forge pathways of healing You cannot take the steps for the person, but you can shine light on the path. By asking the right questions, you can help a person discover for himself or herself the steps to take.

If a person is experiencing denial, don't force the person to look truth square in the face, but probe the options. What if this *were* true; what would you do then?

If a person is in the bargaining stage, promising God all sorts of things, you might merely present the difficulties of those bargains, which might be hard to keep.

If a person is experiencing anger, don't quash it. Promote the venting of these feelings in healthy ways.

If a person is experiencing depression, don't scold the person for this but provide support.

An individual's strength for healing increases exponentially when there are wise and caring friends around. The road to wholeness can be a lot less bumpy.

15

A Quest for Meaning

"It don't mean nuthin'."

We have already discussed this phrase from Vietnam. It was more than a phrase; it was a philosophy, a way of getting through the day.

There was a telling moment early in the intense war film *The Deer Hunter*. Hunting with friends, Robert DeNiro's character holds up a bullet and says, "This is this. This ain't something else. This is this." In other words, there is no meaning beyond the thing itself. You pull the trigger, the bullet moves through the air, the target is struck—nothing to cry about, mope about, mull over. This is merely this.

The depression comes later, when your life has been stripped of all meaning and relationships are shallow and unfulfilling because there is no deep meaning to them. People relate for the moment and move on. This is this. Employment, enjoyment—it's all the same. Weekday, weekend—you push on through. Why? Who knows? Who cares?

Vietnam did a number on our national sense of meaning.

Kennedy idealism sank in the quagmire of Southeast Asia. In the early 1960s, we were rushing out to join the Peace Corps, to make the world a better place. Within the decade, we were torn in two by a controversial war. We were frustrated by our inability to hold the line against communism in one corner of a distant continent. We were sacrificing lives and limbs—and for what? We began to wonder. As we devastated the land we were trying to save, the folly of it all became apparent. For all our sacrifice, it sure seemed we were making the world worse, not better.

Vets came back from Vietnam to an embarrassed America. We had lost, and we didn't want to talk about it. The old codgers at the VFW were still chattering about storming the beach at Normandy, but please don't talk about Saigon. The Vietnam vets began to ask, "Why were we there? Why did we give up our lives for the ideals of a nation that couldn't make up its mind? Is there any meaning in all this?"

Writing about Vietnam vets in *Wounds of War,* Herbert Hendin and Ann Pollinger Haas say:

> Their sense of a war fought without the total commitment of the government or the full support of the American people, their clear lack of understanding of the military or political objectives of the war, and their inability at times simply to identify the enemy, all helped persuade them that there was something casual and unnecessary about the killing and dying in Vietnam. Their attempt to come to terms with the personal meanings of their combat experiences is confounded by their socially shared sense of suspicion and dislocation from a country that to many seemed indifferent about their lives.
>
> For many who fought, the American government's failure to pursue the war to a successful conclusion heightened their feelings that their sacrifices were meaningless.[1]

The mythology of Vietnam was slow to develop. Myths give meaning to hard-to-understand events. Factual or not, they help us explain the unexplainable. But when the Vietnam vets came home, *no one was talking about Vietnam*. The vets had to simmer in their gut-level questions. What was the meaning of it all?

Alcohol and drug abuse ran rampant among Vietnam vets. They still do. An alarming number committed suicide. According to one report, approximately the same number of Vietnam vets have committed suicide since the war as were killed in the war. We have fought a second Vietnam quietly, over the issue of meaning.

The issue of meaning came up at a meeting of the Society for Traumatic Stress Studies. Discussing the recovery processes for Vietnam vets, the assembled psychiatrists and psychologists were freely mentioning the need for meaning. This intrigued me.

I had been educated in an era when such experts avoided this issue. It was considered unprofessional to talk seriously about ultimate meaning, ideas of right or wrong, or moral guilt. These were "religious" matters, unworthy of the attention of scientists.

But there I was, in the midst of well-respected professionals, hearing terms such as "life meaning," "guilt," even "evil" and "forgiveness." Finally, as the only clergyperson in the group, I could no longer restrain myself.

"As I listen to this discussion," I said, "I really wonder whether as mental health professionals you are outside your field now."

There, I'd said it. Like it or not, they would have to get some religious input, wouldn't they? I was expecting some hostility in return, or at least some grumbling resistance. Instead, one psychiatrist said, "You're right. These *are* theological issues. That's why we need you."

Whether we realize it or not, whether we like it or not, any stressful situation reveals much about who we are and our belief systems. Researchers who study trauma, grief, and stress tend to observe only the external responses. As scientists, they are bound by a phenomenological approach: They must concentrate on the phenomena they observe in the patient. But the more they observe, the more they are forced to see their patients as immensely spiritual beings. During combat, a person faces theological issues. Behind the phenomena, behind a person's external behavior, are many ideas about God, even a relationship with God.

Unfortunately, theology is seldom studied in preparation for a degree in psychiatry or psychology. In most secular schools, the subject is still avoided. But at the cutting edge of mental health research, some are seeing the importance of spiritual issues related to treatment.

"When we suffer pain and trauma, the danger of losing a sense of meaning and a guiding purpose in life is especially profound," says psychologist Julius Segal in *Winning Life's Toughest Battles*.[2] That sounds almost religious—"a guiding purpose." The road back to health must be a restoring of that "sense of meaning." We need to find a purpose, a meaning in life that can include the traumatic event just faced.

Viktor Frankl, in his classic work, *In Search of Meaning*, noted, "The search for meaning is the primary force in life."[3] Again, we are in religious territory. The questions of "Why am I here? Where did I come from? What should I be doing?" are normally relegated to churches or synagogues or mosques and theological tomes. But these are the basic underpinnings of our lives, whether we realize it or not. A trauma may shake an assumption we didn't even know we had.

Researchers sometimes call this "cognitive restructuring." When things happen to us that we do not understand, our worldview collapses to some extent. Somehow, we need to restructure our beliefs, to enlarge our belief system to include the event we do not understand.

In *Trauma and Its Wake*, Ronnie Janoff-Bulman summarizes recent research on the stress of victimization:

> Finding a purpose in the victimization is one way of coping
> with a world that makes little sense. . . . Victims often feel

a total lack of comprehension regarding the whys and wherefores of their misfortune. Particularly if they regard themselves as decent people who take good care of themselves and are appropriately cautious, victims are apt to find themselves at a loss to explain why they were victimized.[4]

Recovery happens best when a victim grabs some sort of purpose, even if it's something as simple as "I grew through this," or "I needed to learn this," or "Now I'll be better able to help other victims." These function as suitable explanations that enable the person to put back together some sense of the world as a suitable place to live.

Iraq was not Vietnam. From the start, America's leaders made clear that this military action had meaning. We needed to send troops there to stop the madman Hussein, they said. And they convinced most of us.

But questions of meaning will crop up as we experience the painful aftermath of war. Lost jobs, lost relationships, lost time with families, lost health, lost lives—all these losses will cry out for explanation. Even if we accept a certain national meaning for the events of the Gulf War, we may still search for an ultimate meaning. "Why did God let this happen? Why did it happen to me and my family?"

One soldier had to have his foot amputated when a tank accidentally backed over it. It's one thing to come home a hero, awarded a Purple Heart for a war wound; it's quite another to come home footless due to a meaningless accident. That soldier faces a serious crisis of meaning.

One marine expressed to me his anger at spending eight months on a ship outside Kuwait City. What was their role in this campaign? They were decoys. He could not accept the fact that the battle skills of his unit were wasted on a fake-out. Eight months of his life away from his wife and kids can never be replaced. What was the meaning of it all?

His case gives us an interesting perspective. "Hey," we could say, "don't you see how important you were? It was all part of Schwarzkopf's ingenious plan. The very fact that such a fine amphibious force was poised for attack outside Kuwait City forced the Iraqis to amass their troops there. That opened the inland areas to our attack. It would not have been nearly as successful if you were not there as a decoy. It was all part of Stormin' Norman's grand design."

But after eight frustrating months on a boat, he can't see it. In the middle of a situation, it's hard to see the sense of it.

In any tragedy, there are bound to be those who say, "Don't you see? It's all part of the plan. God has a grand design. It all works together for good."

This may well be true, but in the midst of a trauma, we're like that marine on the boat: We're angry, we're frustrated, and we don't see any sense in it.

Finding Meaning

So what's the answer? Is there an answer? Can we deal with these gnawing questions, or must we rot with despair?

Understand where I'm coming from. I'm operating on two fronts: spiritual and psychological. I'm a chaplain and a counselor. As a Christian minister, I believe there *is* ultimate meaning (though I readily admit I don't always know how to explain it). But as a counselor, I recognize the need for each person to grapple with his or her own questions of meaning. From a psychological perspective, I want to encourage you to make your own journey through the questions and reach a place of peace. But at the same time, I make no bones about the fact that I think Christianity has some answers that can help all of us. With that in mind, drawing both from Christian Scriptures and psychological research, we proceed.

Find meaning in the search for meaning   Why do we ask why? Why do we need to see meaning and purpose in what we do and in what happens to us?

In the concentration camp at Auschwitz during World War II, some Jews were given the task of burying their own dead. Others were given meaningless jobs digging holes and filling them up again. You might think that the act of digging graves would be abhorrent, full of pain and grief, but the grave diggers saw their work as an important gift they could give to their fallen comrades. They found meaning in it. As a result, they had much higher survival rates than those engaged in meaningless labor.

There is something in our essential personhood that longs for direction, purpose, movement toward a goal. Without meaning, there is death.

The Bible speaks of humanity being made ''in the image of God.'' God is presented as a person of purpose, of energy, of movement. His Spirit brings life. In the Hebrew Scriptures, He is personified as Wisdom. In the New Testament, Christ is described as the *Logos,* the Word, the Reason behind all things. God is ultimate meaning.

If we participate in the very nature of God, it only makes sense that we long for meaning in our lives. Only with it do we feel fulfilled.

Let's follow this further. If God is ultimate meaning, then a search for meaning is a search for God. It may be frustrating, even painful, but the search itself draws us closer to the Source of Life.

You may be familiar with the New Testament verse ''All things work together for good . . .'' but the verse goes on, ''. . . to them that love God, to them who are the called according to his purpose'' (Romans 8:28 KJV). The point is that those who are in relationship with God can move closer to Him, even in the most difficult circumstances.

The old story of Job can help us here. In some of the most

brilliant Hebrew poetry, Job and his friends spend thirty-some chapters wondering why God has let things get so bad for this good guy. Then, at the end, God speaks. He talks about His power, the things He has made—*and He doesn't answer Job's questions.* Job never found out why things happened as they did, but he got something even better: the presence of God.

The search for meaning can bring its own meaning.

Reframe your assumptions about reality   This is the cognitive restructuring that I mentioned earlier, but I like the term *reframing* because of the visual imagery. We place a new frame around a picture. Why is this necessary? Well, imagine that the picture is moving, swirling, churning, like one of those Jackson Pollock works (as our lives often are). Suddenly and traumatically, the picture darts outside the frame, leaving a streak of paint on the wall—then another, and another. That's what a trauma does: It violates our borders. It pushes right past the assumptions we use to understand reality. We need to find a bigger frame to embrace the expanding picture.

A kindergarten class was enjoying its art period, working with coloring books. Some were painstakingly following the patterns in the book, carefully pressing their crayons within the heavy black lines. But the teacher came to one student whose crayon strokes were all across the page. "Jimmy," she said, "you're not coloring inside the lines."

The boy looked up and said, "Then draw new lines."

That's what reframing is all about—drawing new lines around reality. We enlarge our assumptions, our beliefs, our expectations, so that we can continue to be at peace with this world.

Earlier, I mentioned the basic assumptions of invulnerability, rationality, justice, and identity that most of us hold. I like to picture this as a circle.

What happens when reality appears outside the circle? We need to draw a larger circle.

Circle of Assumptions

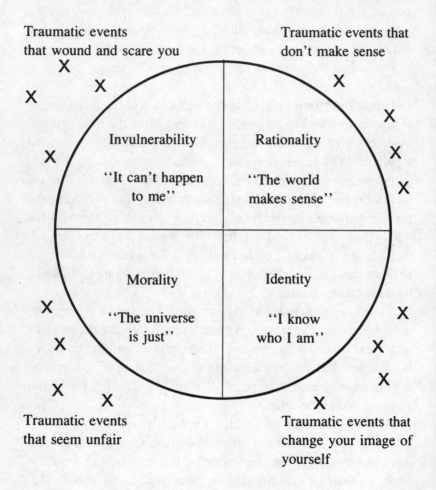

Traumatic events
that wound and scare you

Traumatic events that
don't make sense

Invulnerability

"It can't happen
to me"

Rationality

"The world
makes sense"

Morality

"The universe
is just"

Identity

"I know
who I am"

Traumatic events
that seem unfair

Traumatic events that
change your image of
yourself

Many Christians and devout people of other faiths are among the worst at reframing. The frame around their circle of assumptions has been reinforced by years of religious teaching. They feel confident that God has promised to protect them from all harm. Then a life-threatening injury occurs, and they don't know what to do. They need to stretch that circle, changing their assumption to something like, "God may allow harm to come to me, but He will give me the strength to bear it."

Normal Assumptions	*Expanded Assumptions*
Invulnerability	
God will not let serious harm come to me.	God may allow harm to come to me, but He will give me the strength to bear it.
Rationality	
Everything has to make sense.	There is meaning to everything, though I may not always understand it.
Justice	
Good people get good things; bad people, bad things.	Rewards and punishments will be meted out in the next life. Now it's up for grabs.
Identity	
My identity is defined by my relationships.	I have a unique personhood independent of my relationships.

The larger frame can help us deal with many of life's crises. We can maintain a basic sense of security, sanity, morality, and identity even when buffeted by traumatic events.

Allow for things you don't understand I'm zeroing in on the
area of rationality now, because in that quadrant, the picture
keeps shooting out of the frame. Even with our expanded assumptions, we still get baffled by events. How could there possibly be a meaning to this? If God cares for me even a little, how
could He let this tank run over my foot? Not only do I fail to
pinpoint the reason for my mishap, but I am convinced that there
can be no reason for this mishap; it is so senseless!

As the prophet Isaiah bemoaned the fall of Jerusalem to the
troops of Babylon (from the land that is now Iraq), he wrote,
" 'For my thoughts are not your thoughts, neither are your ways
my ways,' declares the Lord" (Isaiah 55:8). At a certain point,
you just have to to say, "I don't understand what God is up to."

The Apostle Paul reached the same conclusion in his Letter to
the Romans. After wrestling with some painful theological issues, he erupts in (of all things) praise:

> Oh, the depth of the riches of the wisdom and knowledge of
> God!
> How unsearchable his judgments,
> and his paths beyond tracing out!

> Romans 11:33

Then he quotes two passages from the Hebrew Scriptures, the
first from Isaiah, who was questioning the defeat of Jerusalem:

> "Who has known the mind of the Lord?
> Or who has been his counselor?"

> Romans 11:34

And then from Job, who had his own problems:

> "Who has ever given to God,
> that God should repay him?"

> Romans 11:35

In other words, are we in a position to tell God what to do? Does God owe us an explanation?

Finally, Paul presents a benediction: "For from him and through him and to him are all things. To him be the glory forever! Amen" (Romans 11:36).

God Himself is the source, the process, the goal. We may not understand what He's up to, but we can trust that He is there and will continue to be there.

Find meaning in the moment   Interestingly, Paul's Epistle to the Romans goes on to describe ordinary, day-to-day activities by which we can please the Lord. The apostle recognized that the lofty questions of meaning should not be allowed to distract from the regular stuff of life. We must find meaning in each day.

This jibes with psychological research. Among the POWs from Vietnam and the hostages from the Iranian crisis, the ones who fared best were those who put aside the big question of "Why did this happen?" and threw themselves into daily activities that would give meaning to their existence, such as exercises to keep themselves physically fit.

In *Winning Life's Toughest Battles*, Julius Segal writes:

> Few people are able to sustain themselves in the face of crisis only with the belief that "It is God's will"—that there is a higher purpose in human suffering that we cannot perceive. Only rare—and fortunate—individuals find serenity simply by accepting their lot with equanimity and perfect faith. Most of us must find meaning, instead, in the day-to-day activities of our lives.[5]

He quotes Barbara Gordon, who struggled with Valium addiction and a breakdown: "The activity itself is less important than the act of drawing on your own resources, talents, and abilities. Meager and threadbare as you may think these are, it is in the

doing of something meaningful to you that you are enriched; it
fills the emptiness that is so much a part of loss."[6]

While I believe that faith in God's will can be a strong support
for those in crisis, I concur with the need for meaningful action
in our everyday lives. Don't let the big questions of meaning
keep you from doing something that matters *today*.

Touch others Turning your attention outward is a great way to
accomplish this. Trauma tends to isolate people. We feel sure
that no one can know the pain we feel, and to some extent this is
true. But that pain may enable us to sympathize with the pain of
others. In the process of reaching out to them, we may find the
meaning we seek for ourselves.

I spoke with one chaplain who had recently returned from the
gulf. He expressed his anger over the time he had to be away
from his family, but in the next breath he was saying, "I had the
ministry of a lifetime." In a place where everyone was encountering similar struggles, this chaplain could play a key role in
comforting them.

It is often the wounded healer who does the best healing.

16

The Blame Game

We had just moved into a new area that was controlled by the Vietcong. A squad of us went out beyond our perimeter to check and we came under fire. We saw Vietnamese in this grass shack and we started firing. Suddenly a figure moved through the bushes out the back of the grass shack. I shot and it fell. I did not feel anything at first because it was a natural thing to do. We were under fire and it is just instinct. . . . But there were a lot of repercussions after I got out of the service. I had dreams. I still have dreams occasionally. Not just the killing of [this] guy you know, [but] the whole thing in general, all the people I killed. It was sickening. I began to realize they were human beings.[1]

Where do you put the guilt? These Vietnam vets didn't know. In the moment, they did what they felt they had to do. Later, in their dreams, the guilt came back to haunt them.

In the wake of the Gulf War, no one is talking much about guilt yet. It was a popular war, by and large, so we don't want to hear those nagging questions: How many civilians were killed by our bombs? How many of the soldiers we killed were draftees who didn't want to be there?

That's not our fault, we say. We wanted peace, but Saddam kept pushing for war. That may well be true, but it may not quell the nightmares of the soldiers and pilots who did the killing.

Most Americans would rather not think about guilt, sin, or evil. In a world built on the doctrine of "Do your own thing," ideas of right and wrong are tough to apply. Psychiatrist Karl Menninger wrote a book twenty years ago entitled *Whatever Became of Sin?* In it, he wondered whether our easygoing approaches were neglecting an important therapeutic concept: the idea that we humans do evil things for which we need to be forgiven. That's an idea society has continued to overlook, though the psychiatric community has been rediscovering it.

War brings us face-to-face with evil. Human suffering abounds, whether caused by this nation's greed or that person's pride. Combat robs us of innocence. As much as we try to operate in terms of "just wars," war causes devastation to civilians and soldiers alike. A warring nation's motives are usually mixed. For instance, to what extent *were* we fighting for oil? At one point, President Bush remarked that we were fighting to preserve "the American way of life." Just how many miles per gallon does that way of life require? Even though there were legitimate motives in stopping the naked aggression of this Mideast Hitler, it was hard to sort through all our reasons.

Moving from the national level to that of the individual, a soldier or pilot must put aside a bit of his or her moral conscience before going into battle. It is part of the numbing process that enables us to survive. As one army colonel told me, "Listen, I don't want one of my special-forces guys pondering the meaning of life when he puts a knife to someone's throat. If he does, he will more likely end up having his own throat cut!"

Many soldiers confess that they viewed their first human kill as a rite of passage. It marked their growth to manhood through the shedding of another person's blood. At the time, it seemed meaningful. Only later, with time and reflection, does the guilt creep in. *Who was this person I killed? Did he have a family? Why was he there?*

Chaim F. Shatan, founder of the Vietnam Veterans Working Group, writes:

> Veterans will often ask, "How do we turn off the guilt? Can we atone? Why didn't we get killed, rather than carry out illegal orders?" Their own answers follow quickly: They speak of "paying their dues" for surviving unscathed when others did not survive. They invite self-punishment by picking self-defeating fights, inviting rejection from near ones, even getting involved in a remarkably high number of single-car, single-occupant accidents.[2]

Did you catch that language? The vets are talking about "atoning" for their sins. They feel they need to be "punished."

We told the Vietnam vets they were just serving their country, following orders! But rationalization, dehumanization, or denial does not change who we are. Something deep within us knows that it is wrong to take a life. When shed, human blood runs very quickly into a confrontation with God. We are moral beings at heart, no matter how immorally we or our enemy may act. The moral issues do not disappear merely because our commander has told us to forget about morality and follow orders. Neither do moral issues disappear merely because they are out of fashion.

The moral guilt of Vietnam came squeezing out, past all the denial, in the form of nightmares, depression, substance abuse, often suicide. How can we atone for our sins?

The mental health community has few answers for this. One psychiatrist who counsels war veterans told me, "There are many days when I wish I was a priest and could just tell these men, 'You are forgiven.'"

Increasingly, the veteran's perceived need for self-punishment
is being recognized. He realizes he has done something wrong.
No matter how many excuses he has or how legitimate they may
be, he knows he has participated in something awful. Regardless
of how the guilt is rationalized or normalized, the damned spot
does not go away. That guilt is a reminder that we are more than
animals. There is more than a "king of the jungle" ethic at work
here. We humans are moral beings. When this basic morality is
violated, we feel we must be punished—if not by society, then by
ourselves.

Modern treatment is increasingly following a new track. Some
counselors are using a rational therapy technique that gets the vet
to think about what he has done and about how much punishment
he thinks he deserves. "For what you did," a therapist might
ask, "would forty lashes with a whip be sufficient, or ten years
in jail, or having your wife divorce you, or making you drink
yourself to death?" Just what is sufficient punishment for the
moral wrongs committed on or off the killing fields?

This question leads us straight back to the realm of religion, as
my psychiatrist friend admitted in his jesting comment. A priest
can declare the forgiveness of God; what can a shrink do?

Most religions of the world have some concept of penance,
some way to appease the offended deity. Whether it is in keeping
the five pillars of Islam or celebrating Yom Kippur (the Day of
Atonement), this idea of finding forgiveness through penance is
common. As a Christian, I see Jesus as the bearer of all human
punishment. I believe that all our sin and guilt was placed on
Him, that He died in our place so we could enjoy eternal life.
Self-punishment is unnecessary because Jesus has already taken
the blame for our moral wrongs. Our supreme act of penance
comes in putting our trust in Him.

In the Gulf War, only a small percentage of the 550,000 deployed United States troops actually saw combat and had to step
into the killing zones. For many, Desert Storm was pure bore-

dom. These folks will not come home with stories of atrocities hiding in their consciences.

But boredom breeds its own unique kind of moral lapses. When people are taken out of their homeland, placed in a strange land halfway around the world, and stationed in close proximity to others (including many of the opposite sex), many things can happen. Many things did happen.

One medic told me, "I can't believe what happened. I love my wife and kids, and I never believed I could have let happen what happened. But we worked together so closely, and we were just so bored that it just sort of happened. Now that I'm back, the romantic interlude with a young nurse—well, it seems like it was really someone else doing that. It wasn't me—because I'm a happily married man."

The violence of war is not only the violence of killing, it is the violence of seeing yourself do things you never dreamed of doing. Moral lapses are common. Everyone goes a bit crazy in wartime. It seems as if new rules apply. If we are encouraged to behave like raging animals on the battlefield, how do we control ourselves at other times?

Weeks later, months later, maybe years later, the guilt surfaces. "I can't believe I acted like that. What was I thinking? *Was* I thinking?"

What's the cure? Forgiveness.

In *War and the Christian Conscience,* Paul Ramsey notes that up to the year 1000, following the teaching of St. Augustine, a private Christian soldier would have to do forty days of penance for fighting in any war. Even when wars were regularly viewed as holy and just, Augustine recognized the grim realities of combat: Even a just war brings about actions that need forgiveness.

If you go through an airport these days, you're likely to see some member of the armed forces returning from an assignment in the gulf. You may stand next to one as you wait to claim your suitcase. But chances are that the soldier will be carrying some inner baggage as well.

Oh, some may be proud of the way they handled their absence from a husband or wife, boyfriend or girlfriend. Others will have things they don't feel good about. Some will have maintained their moral integrity in combat, but others will have done things they're not proud of. The cameras showed us the way Americans humanely treated the captured Iraqi troops, but war being what it is, and soldiers doing what they are prone to do, there is almost certainly another side to the story. Many soldiers will have shameful secrets.

They need forgiveness from their loved ones, forgiveness from their own hearts, and forgiveness from God.

Claiming Forgiveness

How do you get rid of the guilt?

Some wallow in self-blame for decades, taking every opportunity to punish themselves for what they've done. Others, with proper support from friends or family, can put it away astonishingly easily.

There is usually a "letting go" involved. This is actually pretty easy to do, but extremely difficult to *decide* to do. Imagine a rookie rock climber rappeling down a cliff. He clings tenaciously to one little cleft. "Let go!" his buddies call from above. "The ropes will hold you!" But he isn't absolutely sure that the ropes *will* hold him. All he is sure of is that this small crevice—and his aching fingers—are holding him for now.

Guilt is a way of coping, a crevice in the rock that allows us to keep a certain grip on our ideas of justice in the world. We know exactly where we stand or hang, as the case may be. Our rookie rock climber feels his fingers go numb. He is unable to pull himself up to safety. Now he must trust the ropes.

He lets go. The ropes catch him. He bounces down the face of the cliff and soon stands on solid ground again. "That was easy!" he says, rubbing his fingers, which are no longer numb. "Why didn't I let go sooner?"

Your experience of guilt or that of your loved one may or may not be like hanging on to a rock. I hesitate to say things are easy when I know many who are struggling with these issues. And yet I'm convinced that letting go is the hardest part. Once that decision is made, the healing can begin.

Here are some ideas to help you work through this letting-go process:

Distinguish between fake guilt and real guilt   Many people fake themselves out after a trauma. "I could have saved my brother from that burning building." But the brother was on the third floor, and the stairs were engulfed in flames. Realistically, there was nothing you could have done.

One Vietnam vet was haunted by guilt feelings about his armored vehicle being blown up by a land mine. He was thrown free by the blast, but two men in his command, including the driver, were killed. He felt he should have been driving, *though that was not normally his responsibility.*

A squad leader felt guilt after a Vietcong soldier whom he had captured was pushed out of a helicopter and died. The squad leader was on the ground and had nothing to do with the event, yet he felt responsible. Another event occurred after he returned home. He learned that the squad leader who replaced him had made a tactical error resulting in one soldier's death. *If I were still there,* the original squad leader thought, *that soldier would still be alive.*

Our minds often play tricks like this. They make us feel responsible for things we had nothing to do with. We must sort through these matters logically. It may help to do this with a friend or counselor. Ask what you could have done, reasonably speaking, to change this outcome. To what extent were you responsible? Make as thorough a report as possible to your friend or counselor and trust his or her judgment. You may be carrying unnecessary baggage.

Where there is legitimate guilt, don't downplay it   Once you sort through and discard all the fake guilt, you must come face-to-face with the real guilt. Sometimes our minds can bury the true cause of guilt under layers of phony guilt. When we finally dig through to the real culprit, we may say, "Oh, this is nothing." On the other hand, it may be something too painful to admit, in which case you must have the guts to say, "Yes, I did this, and it was wrong."

This is especially important for loved ones of guilt sufferers to recognize. Most of us want to deny the problem, to excuse it: "Well, it was a war. Everything's fine now. Don't worry about it. You're not a bad person."

We mean well, but this just buries the problem again. The sufferer is likely to say, "You don't understand! You don't *know* how bad I am!" "You don't know what I've done! If you did know, you would despise me!" As long as we deny the magnitude of the sin, we cannot offer meaningful forgiveness.

Forgiveness does not say, "It was nothing." It says, "It was something. It hurt. But it's gone now. All clear."

When we finally zero in on legitimate areas of guilt, our friend or counselor must have the nerve to say, "Yes, you did this, and it was wrong."

Say you're sorry   Are you sorry you did it? Do you feel remorse? Do you wish you could go back and do the right thing? Would you try to make up for it, if possible?

Then say so.

If possible, tell the person you wronged. In many cases that's not possible. So tell yourself, tell God, tell a counselor, tell your spouse or special friend. Put your remorse into words.

The words may have been scurrying around your head for months. Let them out. This will ease the pressure and start you on the path of healing.

Choose an appropriate act of penance or self-punishment
Many war vets feel an acute need for punishment. They have committed crimes against humanity and they are walking free.

In their book *Wounds of War*, Hendin and Haas speak of one vet who was unable to work, acted violently, and had a series of car wrecks. "It was . . . his need to confess and be punished that underlay his symptoms. . . . The remaining therapeutic task was to relieve him of his need for self-destructive atonement."[3]

There's that word again: *atone*. Preachers love to point out that this basically means to be "at one" with someone else, perhaps even with yourself.

The guilt-plagued vet is not at one with his world. He feels estranged from it. He thinks the world cannot fully accept him because of what he has done. It *must* not accept him; if it did, it would have no sense of justice. Woody Allen has that great gag: I wouldn't want to belong to a club that would accept me as a member. The guilty vet says: I wouldn't want to be part of a world that would accept me after what I've done.

The guilt-plagued vet is not at one with his loved ones. He rejects those who want to accept and forgive him. "They can't possibly know how bad I am. I do not deserve their love." The vet seems intent on scaring away those who are closest to him.

The guilt-plagued vet is not at one with himself. Any desire to succeed that he might have is drowned out by a mental chorus saying he doesn't deserve to be happy.

The guilt-plagued vet is not at one with God, believing that God is too holy to care for a sinner like him.

Increasingly, psychiatrists are asking guilt sufferers how much punishment they think they deserve. Facing up to the issue, they can make better decisions. Hendin and Haas wryly observe about their example: "The fifteen-year sentence he had served in a prison of his own making was probably greater than he would have received had he been punished for his combat behavior."

Instead of crashing cars and hitting people, why not sentence yourself to community service? Spend ten hours a week coaching Little League or helping out in an inner-city thrift shop. Pay a fine of 10 percent of your income to a worthy charity. Work out with a counselor or family member what an appropriate sentence might be.

"But," you say, "community service can't begin to pay for the awful things I've done."

Right. That's why I use the word *penance*. It's a word most familiar to Roman Catholics, but I think even many Catholics do not understand it fully.

The concept of penance is based on the idea that we can never fully pay for our sins. We have done too much evil, and God is too perfect. That's why Jesus Christ came to earth. He was wrongly killed after a perfect life, and His death pays for our sins.

So where does penance come in? Well, Christ's punishment applies to our account when we repent—when we tell God we're sorry for our sins. Through Christ, forgiveness is freely offered. But the Bible speaks of the "fruits" of repentance. What are we going to *do* to show that we mean business? Certain acts of prayer and devotion can indicate our willingness to try to live God's way. These acts of penance do not even begin to pay for our sins, but they do show our thankfulness for His forgiveness of us.

And maybe that's what the guilty vet needs. His guilt is so great that even the most oppressive self-punishment would not make up for it. He should simply repent, accept God's forgiveness, and then show God he's sorry by doing something.

Restore relationships If the "crime" you've committed is against your spouse, then you certainly need to restore your marriage as best you can. This will not be easy. You need to weigh your own guilt feelings against the fragility of your marriage. Full disclosure may not yield your desired result, but you may have to do this anyway for your own sanity. In any case, renewed commitment, complete with acts of love, is in order.

It is also possible that you have wronged your friends or family in the act of feeling guilty, perhaps by withdrawing or acting violently. Chances are, these people are ready to forgive you if you are truly interested in restoring the relationship. Just say you're sorry and follow through with appropriate acts of recommitment.

Letting go of your guilt feelings can introduce you to a whole new life.

17

Saying Grace

Go into a bookstore and ask for the self-help section. It may be called "recovery" or something else, but it will be there. You will find shelves packed with books like this one, giving advice.

Many of these books are based at least loosely on a twelve-step program for healing. The twelve steps were developed by the founders of Alcoholics Anonymous, but in recent years they have been adapted to many situations. A foundational part of this healing process is the support group.

There seems to be some therapeutic power in confessing our failures and naming our problems in front of others. There is power in saying, "I am an alcoholic" or "I am a co-dependent." Once we say it, we gain freedom to be ourselves while at the same time expressing our desire to be free from our self-defeating behavior. The self-help group has become the modern world's confessional. People of all faiths are flocking to support groups to find the acceptance, affirmation, and forgiveness they need.

As I have talked with numerous vets returning from the gulf, and with their families, I have noted one common factor: the value of group support. Many of the spouses and families that stayed behind found encouragement in support groups. Those who were deployed forged strong friendships within their units. Often a person's strength in dealing with a crisis was directly related to the strength and cohesion of his or her support group.

"My wife and I had left our church shortly before I was deployed to Saudi," one marine captain told me. "But as soon as I left, the church took her in with some other wives and really ministered to her. She did well because of the mutual support of the other wives. I felt better just knowing she had that group to meet with."

What is the secret of support groups?

Once again, I think the mental health community has backed into a theological concept without knowing it. In the Jewish and Christian Scriptures, two themes regularly emerge: mercy and grace. These are qualities of God that flow out to and through His people. I believe that many of the support groups we see today are actually dispensing mercy and grace, whether they use those terms or not.

Let's take a deeper look at these ideas. When a criminal throws himself on the mercy of the court, what is he doing? He is admitting his crime and asking society to accept him anyway. That's essentially what happens in a twelve-step support group. A person says, "I am an alcoholic [or whatever]. Please accept me and help me move forward."

Quite often, there is good reason *not* to accept the person. He or she has a problem or may have done bad things. But mercy accepts the person in spite of the problem.

Theologically speaking, this is true of God as well. When the Scriptures speak of God being "rich in mercy," this means He is willing to accept us in spite of our sins. That same quality comes through in people who try to follow God's way. "Blessed are the merciful," Jesus said, "for they shall obtain mercy" (Matthew 5:7 KJV). This simple statement indicates the relationship-building aspect of mercy. If I accept you, you can accept me. As I open up to you about my problems and seek your mercy, I am more willing to show mercy when you tell me of your problems. The tide of mercy washes back and forth.

Grace has a slightly different angle. I define it as "a joyous favor." Usually when theologians get hold of this word, they squeeze the joy right out of it. But in the Scriptures, grace is gift giving; it is celebration; it is blessing.

Support groups can be fun. They *should* be fun. Not only do their members accept one another and affirm one another, but they *enjoy* one another, give themselves to one another, and celebrate together. This is grace.

Grace turns a negative into a positive. Grace says, "If I never had this problem, I would never have met all you great people." There is a deep truth here that can help us find our way in this topsy-turvy world: We are strongest when we are weak.

Have you ever played with one of those woven knuckle grabbers? They're small cylinders made out of basket-weaving material or something like that. You put a finger in each end and pull. The harder you pull, the tighter it gets. The strongest person gets frustrated, because his strength is just working against him. The secret is to give in, to ease up, to be weak. Then the fibers relax and you can pull your fingers out easily.

Life is like that. Bull your way through your problems in your own strength, and they'll just get worse. But admit your weakness to others and you will find new strength. The community of the weak can celebrate together.

A medical services officer from the gulf told me of a number of people who just couldn't adapt to life in the desert. The pressures were just too great. They were sent home.

More often than not, he said, these were the loners. They hadn't connected with others. They had no support group in which to experience mercy and grace. Yet most of the other soldiers did connect. In the barracks, in the VCR tent, at the chaplain's meetings, they found the acceptance and support they needed.

Finding Grace

How can you find this mercy and grace for yourself?

Find or form a support group   Do not underestimate the need to get together with others who have had similar experiences. If you're the spouse of a gulf vet, do not feel excluded or inadequate if your loved one joins a group. No matter how much compassion you may bring to the relationship, there is a special value in sharing with those who have *been there*. Find your own support group to help yourself and learn to help your loved one.

About a year after the Delta crash, I talked to one member of the cleanup crew who had been among the first to go through the wreckage. He had seen the most gruesome sights imaginable. Ever since, he had been haunted by those memories.

"Was anybody else with you," I asked, "when you went through the wreckage?"

"Yeah, there was one other guy."

"Have you talked to him at all?"

"Naw, he moved away after that."

"Why don't you give him a call?"

He did call his old colleague, and he found that the other guy had also been burdened by gruesome memories. Together, they could vent some steam, share the burden, and ease it a little.

Resources (page 189) lists various organizations you can call for postwar help.

If the idea of a support group sounds too "shrinkish" to you, then just make it a point to keep in touch with some of your gulf pals. If there are some in the area, invite them over occasionally. You don't want to live in the past, but you can use friends from the past to cleanse old wounds. If you have uniquely gulf-related problems or things you find difficult to talk about, you may want to exclude your spouse from such "reunions." This must be done with communication and grace on both parts. In other situations, including your spouse can be a great way to draw him or her into the network of friends you made in the gulf.

Be honest about your needs and problems Whether you are meeting with a support group or just dealing with an old friend one-to-one, you must be honest about your feelings. There is no value in putting on the "strong" act. True strength comes from expressing your feelings and dealing with them. It shows true courage to admit you have emotional needs.

Do not fear rejection or embarrassment. If for some reason another person does make light of your needs, that's his problem. He's not playing by the rules. If you think a fear of rejection is keeping you from being honest with your friends, this might be a good reason to seek out an organized support group. In that structure, the "rules" of honesty and acceptance are more thoroughly applied.

Accept others This is the flip side of honesty. If you have to muster your courage to open up to others, remember that the others are mustering their courage, too. Don't squelch this.

Acceptance may be difficult for a person whose spouse returns from the gulf as a very different person. *Is this the same person I married?* But remember that we are all changing. The returning spouse may find that the spouse at home has changed, too, gaining new abilities or interests. Accept these changes and celebrate them, then commit yourself to plot new courses of change *together* in the future.

Have fun Remember the joyous side of grace. Enjoy the people you meet with. Enjoy the people closest to you.

We all have a tendency to focus on our problems. Our nightmares, physical difficulties, and relationship woes keep us from living life as we want to. When we are always thinking about our problems, that magnifies them. They become like a loose tooth one is always prodding with the tongue. The continual attention just makes it looser and makes the problem worse.

Can we look past the problems and enjoy life anyway? That's true grace.

Robert Schuller uses the phrase, **"Turn your scars into stars"** This is a crucial concept presented in a catchy form.

Everyone has problems. Major or minor, some sort of difficulty afflicts each one of us. The people who thrive—and I'm not talking about making tons of money or running a major corporation—the people who live life to the fullest are those who turn their problems around and even capitalize on them.

One of my friends, Greg Nelson, writes and arranges songs. Years ago, he went to South America with Christian singer Keith Green. There he got a parasitic infection that later robbed him of his sight. The doctors told him it was permanent. What an awful event!

In the following months, Greg and his wife began to prepare for a life of blindness. He studied Braille and so on. But within the year, his sight returned. In that period of literal darkness, God turned Greg's life around. His music career found new energy. Among the songs he wrote was the hauntingly simple "People Need the Lord." That was the crux of the truth he learned. The glamor, the excitement of the music industry, all paled in significance next to the greatest human need—a relationship with God.

I don't want to give you pie-in-the-sky answers here. If you have a problem in the wake of the Gulf War, it's tough. It hurts. But I believe it is possible to go through this dark tunnel and emerge on the other side as a stronger, more rooted, more centered person. Work through the present crisis and find an exciting new direction in it.

Jesus loved to tell stories. In Luke 15, there are three stories, all dealing with lostness.

First there is the lost sheep. A shepherd counts only 99 of his flock of 100, so he searches high and low and finally finds the missing creature. Then he calls his neighbors and friends and says, "Rejoice with me; I have found my lost sheep."

Then there's the lost coin. A woman loses one of her ten silver coins and sweeps her house thoroughly until she finds it. "Rejoice with me," she asks her neighbors. "I have found my lost coin."

Finally there is the lost son. You may know him as the Prodigal. He takes his share of the family fortune and leaves home, squandering it all, ending up on a pig farm. There he comes to his senses and returns to his father, who waits with open arms. "Quick!" the father says. "Let's have a feast and celebrate. For this son of mine was dead and is alive again; he was lost and is found."

I don't know what you lost in the Gulf War. Family time? Personal innocence? Perhaps something as serious as your own health or the life of a loved one?

Mercy is all about admitting what you've lost and what you need. It's the kid in the pigsty realizing what he has to do. It's the father who goes out to the road every day to look for his son and welcomes him as a prince when he returns. Grace is all about rediscovering what you have lost—or maybe something even better—and finding a reason to dance.

Appendix

Common Questions Raised About the Gulf War

As a chaplain do you think the Gulf War was a "just war"?

People have debated the rightness and wrongness of war for ages. The Greeks were probably the first to argue for some sense of justice in determining whether to go to war and then waging a war justly once it was in process. Many of the Greek criteria were picked up in the early history of the church. Throughout the ages, Christian theologians have argued that certain criteria must be met in order for a war to be considered just. But before looking at these criteria, let me first give an overview of several different "Christian" positions. I put Christian in quotes because many would not see all of these as Christian positions, but I do. I have many brothers in the faith who hold these positions strongly, and I appreciate their stances, even though I may not hold them myself.

First, some Christians hold what might be called an "activist" position. They argue that the Bible (particularly Romans 13) teaches that Christians are to obey the government and the government has the right to bear the sword. This would include using the sword of state in military warfare. If the president or king says to go to war, then the Christian should obey, because God will hold both the ruler and the citizens accountable for their actions. I know of many churches around active-duty bases that not only prayed for the safety and quick return of our troops from the gulf but also prayed for the success of our troops, to the point of even capturing and/or killing Saddam Hussein. These are activists!

Other Christians take another road: They are pacifists. They center their belief in Jesus' command to "turn the other cheek" and see their primary responsibility as not to the government but to God. God's law supersedes man's laws and wars. The Christian must not bear arms, seek retaliation, or put himself in any situation where he might have to take life. I know some Christians who argue that the government's only reason to go to war should be to protect American lives on American soil. In all other situations, these people are pacifists.

The third option is what has normally been called the "just-war" tradition. This position says that some wars are just and some are not. This view admits that the taking of life and waging of war is less than ideal, even sinful, but it also bears witness to the reality that sometimes a greater injustice is done by allowing evil to reign. Just-war principles seem to exist in Genesis 14, when Abraham took arms in order to rescue his nephew Lot. They are also seen in Deuteronomy 20, where peace is desired and offered until peace is rejected. Then armed force is authorized. In the history of the tradition, the most consistent criteria are: just cause, just intention, last resort, formal declaration, limited objectives, proportionate means, and noncombatant immunity.

Now let's see how many of these criteria can be seen in the Gulf War. Kuwait was invaded by a hostile nation with hostile intent. Once they were in the country, peace-oriented means were attempted to restore the region to peace. However, Hussein rejected all peace proposals. At some point in any situation, someone must determine that enough is enough, and then go to last-resort thinking. Even though I would have preferred the United States Congress to have declared war according to the Constitution (Article 1, section 8), at least it did vote for formal approval of the president's position. This seems to satisfy the requirement of formal declaration. The objective from day one of the war was limited to removing the Iraqi troops from Kuwait. Even though from our afterwar perspective it might seem to have been better to have marched into Baghdad and dealt with Hussein once for all, at least the United States *was* pursuing limited objectives.

The issue of proportionate means will always be hotly debated. The question, as always, is who gets to decide! Any war deals with violence. Even one person being killed is violence to the family and friends of the one who was lost. Whether the damage done to Iraq was necessary to get the job done, and no more, will be debated and probably left for scholarly discussion in the years to come. However, I believe we did not do all we could have done and were always holding back in principle, both to protect our own soldiers and to save as many innocents as possible.

The issue of target discrimination was probably the clearest. In no war has there been more ability to discriminate targets and hit them with extreme accuracy. Yes, some civilians were killed. In every war, some innocents and civilians are killed, but the question is, are they targeted as such? When command posts are located intentionally in hospitals, schools, and hotels, some civilians will be killed if those targets are eliminated. But I had the distinct impression that General Schwarzkopf constantly was concerned about not killing the true innocents and civilians.

So, from these criteria, you may decide for yourself whether you think this war was just. Of course, just because there exists just cause does not mean we should jump into any war. Every day there is some injustice going on in the world, but whether or not we commit our troops also depends on our alliances in the world, balance-of-power issues or strategic interests, and how we perceive our stewardship as a world power. These are tough issues for some religious people who desire black-and-white resolution. But our world is very complex today.

While I was in the gulf, I had a brief romantic encounter while on board ship. Now that I'm back, should I tell my spouse?

To tell or not to tell. That is the question. This is a very common question. In the air force, we have a saying: "What happens on the other side of the pond stays on the other side of the pond." But as a chaplain and counselor, I know that things do not stay "on the other side of the pond." I have heard many confessions in the back of C-130s and 141s, coming back from overseas deployments. People ask the same question. Should I tell my wife or girlfriend (or nowadays husband or boyfriend)?

The first question I ask in return is, "How good a forgiver is your partner?" The second is, "Do you think your relationship is strong enough to survive this news?" The third question is often, "Do you value your marriage and want to keep it together?" You see, I believe in the permanency of marriage. I also believe that true intimacy has open and honest communication. But we do not live in an ideal world. Some spouses can handle unfaithfulness, some can't. People and marriages are all different. Some people have a great ability to forgive and move on; others don't. What I encourage is some realistic appraisal of the marriage and the counsel of good friends, with the desire that *ultimately* the person will be capable of full disclosure.

My husband was in Saudi for almost eight months, saw limited combat, and he says he saw some gruesome things. Does this mean he will have problems? I haven't seen any yet.

Your concern is justified. Spouses and employers are often the first to notice visible changes in a person affected by the stress of war. I think the key is to encourage him to talk to someone about what he saw. This may not be you. He may feel more comfortable talking about it to another vet or someone who saw exactly what he saw. But you can certainly communicate to him that you want to hear about it. On the other end of the spectrum, don't be looking for reactions when there are none. I suspect many of the troops will return unscathed and do fine reintegrating with normal life. This book tells you of some behavioral and emotional symptoms to be aware of. If they are not present, don't worry about them until there is something to deal with.

While I was overseas, my wife took care of the finances. But when I got back, everything was a disaster. Bills were unpaid and long overdue, and most of our savings were gone. On an E-3 pay rate, I don't earn that much money. What can I do?

First, I would recommend talking to your first sergeant. That's the place to begin in the military. Most units have some benevolence funds that can be tapped for special cases. Your first shirt can take your need to your commander, if necessary. Also, the armed forces have their own funds for financial assistance. In the air force it is the Air Force Aid Society. If you are a National Guardsman, check on your own state level for financial assistance. If you are on an active-duty base, check with your family assistance office, which can put you in contact with a whole array of services, including the American Red Cross. Also, most of the credit agencies have worked with Desert Storm families with much patience. Call each of your creditors and tell them your situation. See if they will waive overdue fees or interest. Most understand the situation and will help you work out a payment plan that is reasonable for you.

When I left for the gulf, I gave power of attorney to my fiancée. But while I was away, we broke up. Now I find out she sold some of my things. What can I do to try to get them back?

Powers of attorney are powerful. It is a total transferral of power. Since this is a legal question, contact your Judge Advocate (attorney). However, I predict the news he will give you will not be good. All units should have made it very clear what signing the power of attorney meant: You were giving power to whoever was named in the document to act totally in your name. If a car was owned in your name, a power of attorney would grant that person the legal right to sell the car in your name. It's all legal. The good news is, you were probably right to break off the engagement!

I'm one of the marines who were on board the amphibious assault ships just off Kuwait City. Since we saw no action and were only functioning as "decoys," I can't understand why I feel so numb and angry since coming back.

You marines had a very unusual situation. You sat for a very long time with the anticipation of being the first to the action. The sitting alone was enough to breed numbness. Your body adjusted to the routine, and it will take some time to readjust to your normal routine. As marines you are gung-ho, semper-fi, always ready and faithful. All of your training is geared toward being where the action is, but in this war, you were the decoys. Others might take the ribbons and run, but not a marine; marines earn their medals. You played a very important part in the war (being the decoy), and it worked. But you weren't allowed to see action and prove your stuff. I don't think your anger is wrong. It will pass. Be thankful you are alive and back home. Pin the medals on with pride. Someday you'll tell your grandkids about how exciting the whole experience was—and you've got the ribbons to prove it!

I'm a reservist who got activated for my job specialty. However, after being in Saudi for just two weeks, I was sent home. I think it was because I outranked my active-duty counterpart. Any comments?

I've heard variations of this experience several times. In this war, reserve and active-duty personnel served side by side, fulfilling the daily mission. However, in any war, personality and politics are never eliminated. The active duty's concern for cutbacks after the war was probably a factor in not allowing the reservists to "shine" too well or be involved to such an extent that the active-duty role would be questioned by Congress. Reservists unfortunately are viewed as part-timers because they *are* part-timers. Hopefully, we will learn from this war not only where the total force concept broke down but more important, where it worked and worked well.

One member of my unit was killed by friendly fire. I know these things happen in war, but this seems so senseless. I just can't put it behind me.

Even though we all know these things happen in warfare, they really don't hit us until it happens to someone we know. I would be more concerned about you if you felt nothing. First, I would suggest forgiving the pilot who innocently launched his rocket at a friendly. He has his own trauma to live with the rest of his life. Forgiveness is a process. Every time the event comes to mind again, you need to say, "I forgive you for killing my buddy." Second, many Vietnam vets have told me how therapeutic it has been for them to contact the relatives of their buddies. Write a note, call, or visit personally the ones who are grieving the most. Tell them how much you valued their loved one's friendship or what you most enjoyed about him. Remember, these people cannot move on in their lives until they have finished grieving for their loved ones. You can be part of their healing as you further your own.

This war seemed to raise women's issues to new levels. Women were killed, taken captive, and left small babies in the arms of husbands and other relatives. What do you think about women in combat?

Certainly, since the civil rights movements of the late sixties and early seventies, the entire gender complexion of the military has changed. I must say at the outset, as a chaplain, that I have increasing concern about the single-parent issue. It is true that single parents are supposed to keep up-to-date authorization cards as to who will care for their children if they are mobilized. However, I don't think most bases were realistically prepared for all the issues facing the dilemmas of single parents. Many single parents were frankly surprised that the government would actually mobilize them, even though the service never pretended otherwise. More discussion and preparation needs to take place in peacetime. On the issue of women in combat zones, I have heard nothing but positive comments. One medic told me his commander was a woman. The only thing she couldn't do was carry the very heavy stretchers. Other than that, she was very professional and competent. One army officer said there were no more complaints from women than from the men. In fact, everyone complained. "We all hung in there and did our jobs, but we all complained." The women's issue in the military is just a part of the larger question of women's opportunities and roles in our society. The reality now is that they are in the military with increasing responsibility and involvement. Where one draws the line, and why, becomes very much a political statement of our larger social values. These are no easy issues.

How do you think the war with Iraq will affect the Vietnam vets?

I think the Gulf War can be both good news and bad news for the Vietnam vets. Just as many of the Rambo-type movies can remind vets of their wartime experience, so the coverage of this war can and will. And some of these memories will be painful.

But there's another principle we should be aware of: Vets need vets. In American Legion halls and VFW buildings, World War II vets eat and drink with Korean and Vietnam vets and mentor one another through their wartime experiences. With this war just ending, there will exist a new opportunity for Vietnam vets to mentor this younger group into the veteran experience.

Personally, I have been pleased to see the number of Vietnam vets being included in the parades. This is excellent therapy for both generations of vets. However, I have heard of other reactions to the parades. Some Vietnam vets have been saying things like, "This was not even a real war, so why are these new vets getting such acclaim, when so few of them actually put their lives on the line? What's a ground war of two days, compared to 300 days or more in Nam? It shows how much our society is still screwed up." These vets continue to fight the war in their heads. Now is a time for healing, and Vietnam vets can lead the way.

As a Christian chaplain, how did you feel about defending a Muslim country and having to work with Muslims who prevented you from wearing the cross on your uniform?

This policy was held by the Saudis at the beginning of the deployment. By the end, chaplains were openly conducting Christian services, distributing Bibles, and wearing their crosses.

Even though I understand the Saudis' public gesturing about protecting their holy places and trying to save face with their Arab neighbors by not admitting that Christianity is openly practiced in their country, I think they were wrong. When they ask the help of a Judeo-Christian nation, they cannot ask that its spiritual resources and advisers be limited or barred from the deployment. Everyone knows that Aramco has had Christian services and chaplains for their employees for years. Christianity has been and continues to be practiced in Saudi Arabia, so this posturing was nothing but a sham.

Even though early attempts were made to restrain chaplains, the chaplain corps will never be totally restrained. Our calling is to a ministry of presence. Whether we are called chaplains or morale officers or support personnel, we know who we are and why we are there. The Gospel in the life of a chaplain cannot be restrained. I know one chaplain who wrote CHAPLAIN in large white letters across his helmet. Another chaplain put a fish, the oldest symbol of Christianity, on his helmet and tent. As chaplains, our commitment is to being where the greatest need is. Whether or not we can wear the cross or the tablets on our uniforms, we are there to minister to the spiritual needs of our men and women, and it will be done. In the terrorist attack on the Lebanon marine corps barracks, only one chaplain was left alive and uninjured. One photojournalist caught the spirit of what the military chaplaincy is all about. The photo showed a rabbi, having taken off his skullcap, wiping the face of a young marine who was still very much buried in the debris. That's the chaplaincy! We do what needs to be done.

Do you have any final thoughts about this Middle East war? It seems the Arabs are fighting a holy war against all infidels, and that includes both Christians and Jews.

I sincerely hope that the alliance formed against Iraq will demonstrate to some Arab nations that the United States is not the "Satan America" that some Islamic groups have claimed. The Arab world must move beyond using and abusing the Israel question. If their concern is truly for the Palestinians, then surely they could get their petrodollars working toward a more legitimately recognized political movement. Likewise, if Israel truly wants peace, then they must be prepared to give something up. Overall, the Middle East is a tragic testimony to world power domination. At the same time, it seems to me that whoever moves in to "fix" the Middle East ends up losing, and losing big. My favorite illustration of the region goes like this:

A scorpion was once sitting on a rock by the Sea of Galilee. A fish poked his head out of the water to look at the scorpion. The scorpion said to the fish, "Let me jump on your back, and take me to the other side of the lake. That way I won't have to walk around in the hot sun."

The fish replied, "But you are a scorpion; you would sting me, and I would die."

The scorpion answered, "Yes, but scorpions do not swim. If I did that, we would both die."

The fish thought about it and said, "That makes sense. Get on my back, and I'll take you." The scorpion jumped on the back of the fish, and off they went. When they got to the middle of the sea, the scorpion stung the fish. The fish looked around, and with a final gasp said, "Now why did you do that? We are both going to die!"

Trying to tread water, the scorpion yelled, "Because this is the Middle East!"

Every time I go to the Middle East or read another book about it, the more convinced I become about the reality of that parable. Does this mean that we should stop trying to work for peaceful solutions? Certainly not. Does this mean a lasting peace is possible? Probably not. Personally, I do not believe there will be a lasting peace in the world (including the Middle East) until the Prince of Peace comes from heaven to establish it. Until then, we are to work for peaceful relations among all people and continue to pray for the peace of Jerusalem. We should not completely lay down either our plowshares or our swords. We should keep both fairly well honed and sharp.

Source Notes

Chapter 1 The Preparation

1. *Reader's Digest*, April 1991, p. 84.
2. *Vogue*, December 1990, p. 301.
3. *Reader's Digest*, op. cit.
4. *Vogue*, op. cit.
5. *Reader's Digest*, April 1991, p. 86.
6. Compiled from *Reader's Digest*, op. cit., and *The New Republic*, March 25, 1991, p. 20.
7. Laura R. Blumenfeld, "Living on the Edge of Conflict," *New York Times Magazine*, September 9, 1990, p. 52.
8. *People*, February 18, 1991, p. 40.
9. Blumenfeld, op. cit.
10. *Vogue*, op. cit.
11. *Newsweek*, January 28, 1991, p. 38.
12. *Life*, March 1991, p. 86.
13. The *New York Times*, January 15, 1991, p. B1.
14. *Life*, op. cit.
15. *Industry Week*, February 18, 1991, p. 67.
16. *Time*, January 28, 1991, p. 37.

Chapter 2 The Battle

1. *People*, January 28, 1991, p. 36.
2. *U.S. News & World Report*, February 4, 1991, p. 54.

3. The *New York Times*, January 15, p. B1.
4. *People*, January 28, 1991, p. 38.
5. *Newsweek*, January 28, 1991, p. 38.
6. *People*, January 28, 1991, p. 42.
7. Ibid., p. 30.
8. *Newsweek*, January 28, 1991, p. 31.
9. Stewart M. Powell, "Voices From the War," *Air Force* magazine, April 1991, p. 38.
10. *Macleans*, January 28, 1991, p. 28.
11. Powell, "Voices."
12. Ibid.
13. Ibid.
14. The *New York Times*, January 17, 1991, p. A1.
15. Ibid., p. A19.
16. Eric Schmitt, "Computerized Accuracy," The *New York Times*, January 19, 1991, p. 6.
17. The *New York Times*, January 18, 1991, p. A15.
18. *Time*, January 28, 1991, p. 37.
19. The *New York Times*, January 18, 1991, p. A15.
20. Powell, "Voices."
21. Ken and Joan Hendren, *Trumpet of Salvation*, prayer letter.
22. *The New Republic*, February 11, 1991, p. 21.
23. The *New York Times*, January 23, 1991, p. A10.
24. *Philadelphia Inquirer*, March 21, 1991, p. 1-B.
25. John Malthaner, "Acts of Heroism," *National Guard*, May 1991, p. 30.
26. *The New Republic*, February 11, 1991, p. 21.
27. *U. S. News & World Report*, February 4, 1991, p. 54.
28. *The New Republic*, February 11, 1991, p. 22.
29. *U.S. News & World Report*, February 4, 1991, p. 54.
30. *The New Republic*, February 11, 1991, p. 14.
31. Chapel of the Air, "Operation Desert Storm Prayer Guide."
32. *People*, February 18, 1991, pp. 40–41.
33. Ibid., p. 40.
34. Ibid., p. 43.

Chapter 3 The Victory

1. Ken and Joan Hendren, *Trumpet of Salvation*, prayer letter.
2. *Time*, February 18, 1991, pp. 15–18.
3. *The New Republic*, March 11, 1991, p. 27.
4. *Time*, February 25, 1991, p. 37.
5. *Newsweek*, March 4, 1991, p. 28.

6. *Newsweek*, March 4, 1991, p. 29.
7. *Time*, February 25, 1991, p. 37.
8. *Newsweek*, February 11, 1991, p. 30.
9. *Newsweek*, March 4, 1991, p. 30.
10. Ibid., p. 31.
11. Ibid., p. 30.
12. Nancy Gibbs, "Life on the Line," *Time*, February 25, 1991, p. 36.
13. *Newsweek*, March 11, 1991, p. 48.
14. The *New York Times*, February 25, 1991, p. A13.
15. *Time*, March 11, 1991, pp. 27, 30.
16. *The New Republic*, March 25, 1991, p. 25.
17. *Newsweek*, March 11, 1991, p. 45.
18. Ibid., p. 46.
19. *People*, March 18, 1991, p. 42.
20. *Newsweek*, March 11, 1991, p. 48.
21. *People*, March 18, 1991, p. 42.
22. *The New Republic*, March 25, 1991, p. 25.
23. *The New Republic*, April 1, 1991, p. 14.
24. Ibid.
25. *People*, March 18, 1991, pp. 44–46.
26. *Newsweek*, May 6, 1991, p. 61.
27. *USA Today*, April 30, 1991, p. 1A.
28. *Newsweek*, May 6, 1991, pp. 60–61.
29. *USA Today*, March 18, 1991, p. 2A.
30. Ibid.
31. Ibid.
32. *Philadelphia Inquirer*, March 31, 1991, p. 5-E.
33. The *New York Times*, April 28, 1991, p. 1.

Chapter 5 Like Nothing We've Ever Seen

1. *Philadelphia Inquirer*, May 12, 1991, pp. 1, 8-A.
2. Gregg Easterbrook, "Robowar," *The New Republic*, February 11, 1991, p. 17.
3. The *New York Times*, March 11, 1991, p. A11.
4. Ibid.
5. Ibid.
6. The *New York Times*, January 22, 1991, p. C8.
7. *Time*, April 1, 1991, p. 82.
8. *The New Republic*, March 25, 1991, p. 8.
9. The *New York Times*, March 11, 1991, p. A11.

Chapter 6 How Bad Is It?

1. S. Futterman and E. Pumpian-Mindlin, *PTSD Research Quarterly*, Winter 1991, pp. 3–4.
2. Richard I. Ridenour, *Journal of the American Medical Association* 265:5 (February 6, 1991): 559.
3. *Philadelphia Inquirer*, May 12, 1991, pp. 1, 8-A.

Chapter 7 Nostalgia: War Trauma Through the Ages

1. As quoted in *Harper's*, February 1991, pp. 26–28.

Chapter 8 Dealing With Loss

1. *USA Today*, March 25, 1991, p. 2A.

Chapter 9 On the Balance Beam

1. Vicki E. Hogancamp and Charles R. Figley, "War: Bringing the Battle Home," *Stress and the Family*, vol. 2 (New York: Brunner/Mazel, 1983), p. 156.

Chapter 10 Family Matters

1. *The Record*, Hackensack, New Jersey, March 24, 1991, p. L-1.
2. *USA Today*, March 18, 1991, pp. 1–2A.
3. The *New York Times*, April 1, 1991, p. A10.
4. *Philadelphia Inquirer*, May 12, 1991, pp. 1, 8-A.
5. Ibid.
6. *The Record*, March 24, 1991, pp. L-1, 16.

Chapter 11 Economic Sanctions

1. The *New York Times*, March 23, 1991, p. 29.
2. Ibid., p. 41.
3. *Philadelphia Inquirer*, March 31, 1991, p. 5-E.

Chapter 12 The Next Stage Leaves in Ten Minutes

1. Robert D. Parlotz, USAFR, "Dealing with Combat Inquiries and Death/ Dying," MAC Readiness/Mobility Training Materials, Scott AFB, Illinois.

Chapter 14 Regaining Control

1. Julius Segal, *Winning Life's Toughest Battles* (New York: McGraw-Hill, 1986), p. 9.
2. Charles R. Figley and Hamilton I. McCubbin, eds., *Stress and the Family*, vol. 2 (New York: Brunner/Mazel, 1983), p. 11.

Chapter 15 A Quest for Meaning

1. Herbert Hendin and Ann Pollinger Haas, *Wounds of War* (New York: Basic Books, 1984), pp. 47–48.
2. Julius Segal, *Winning Life's Toughest Battles* (New York: McGraw-Hill, 1986), p. 55.
3. Viktor Frankl, *In Search of Meaning* (New York: Washington Square Press, 1959), p. 11.
4. Ronnie Janoff-Bulman, "The Aftermath of Victimization: Rebuilding Shattered Assumptions," in Charles R. Figley, ed., *Trauma and Its Wake* (New York: Brunner/Mazel, 1985), p. 21.
5. Segal, *Winning*, p. 71.
6. Barbara Gordon, "You Can Begin Again," *Parade,* December 30, 1984, pp. 4–6.

Chapter 16 The Blame Game

1. Robert S. Laufer, Ellen Frey-Wouters, and Mark S. Gallops, "Traumatic Stressors in the Vietnam War and Post-traumatic Stress Disorder," in Charles R. Figley, ed., *Trauma and Its Wake* (New York: Brunner/Mazel, 1985), pp. 78–79.
2. Chaim F. Shatan, "Stress Disorders Among Vietnam Veterans: The Emotional Context of Combat Continues," in Charles R. Figley, ed., *Stress Disorders Among Vietnam Veterans* (New York: Brunner/Mazel, 1978), p. 48.
3. Herbert Hendin and Ann Pollinger Haas, *Wounds of War* (New York: Basic Books, 1984), p. 87.

Resources

Organizations and Individuals*

American Association for Counseling and Development
5999 Stevenson Avenue
Alexandria, Virginia 22304

Dr. Melvin Jacob
V.A. Medical Center and Medical College of Georgia
Augusta, Georgia

Grace Marad, R.N.
John Brock
Vietnam Vet Center
103 Liberty Street
Manchester, New Hampshire 03104

Cpt. Paul Bartone, Ph.D.
Department of Military Psychiatry
Walter Reed Army Institute of Research
Washington, DC 20307

Harvey Hilbert, Ph.D.
Stress Intervention Center
8748 Brecksville Road
Brecksville, Ohio 44141

Department of Military Medicine
Uniformed Services University of the Health Sciences
Bethesda, Maryland 20814

Jeffrey Mitchell, Ph.D.
Emergency Health Services Department
University of Maryland Baltimore County
Catonsville, Maryland 21228

William Kelleher, Ph.D.
Chief, Behavioral Health Psychology
Wilford Hall, USAF Medical Center
San Antonio, Texas 78236

Life Counseling Services
63 Chestnut Road
Paoli, Pennsylvania 19301

Department of Clinical Social Work
Timberlawn Psychiatric Hospital
4645 Samuell Boulevard
Dallas, Texas 75228

Counseling and Readjustment Services
"A Center for Stress Recovery"
914 Richland Street, Suite A-102
Columbia, South Carolina 29201

The National Center for PTSD (Post-Traumatic Stress Disorder)
VAM & ROC 116D
White River Junction, Vermont 05009

The Society for Traumatic Stress Studies
435 N. Michigan Avenue, Suite 171
Chicago, Illinois 60611-4067

*The organizations and individuals listed are those with which the author has had professional acquaintance or working experience in the field of wartime stress or wartime-type stress. The first place for people needing information or help connected with the aftermath of Desert Storm should be their own mental health officer in their unit. For family and friends, contact should be made with the nearest Veterans Administration hospital. In addition, the local mental health professions should be contacted, but ask for someone who has dealt with or specialized in combat stress reactions. This is a relatively new field, and not all mental health professionals have had specific training in combat reactions and the resultant family stress.

Bibliography

Burkle, F.M.; Sanner, P.; and Wolcott, B.W., eds. *Disaster Medicine*. New York: Medical Examination Publishing Co., Inc., 1984.

Chandler, Jerome Greer. *Fire and Rain*. Austin: Texas Monthly Press, 1986.

Davidson, A.D. "Air Disaster: Coping With Stress, A Program That Worked." *Police Stress*, Spring 1979, 20 22.

Figley, Charles R., ed. *Stress Disorders Among Vietnam Veterans*. New York: Brunner/Mazel Publishers, 1978.

————. *Trauma and Its Wake: The Study and Treatment of Post-Traumatic Stress Disorder*. New York: Brunner/Mazel Publishers, 1985.

Figley, Charles R., and McCubbin, Hamilton. *Stress and the Family: Coping With Catastrophe*. New York: Brunner/Mazel Publishers, 1983.

Frankl, Viktor E. *Man's Search for Meaning*. New York: Washington Square Press, 1959.

Hendin, Herbert, and Hass, Ann Pollinger. *Wounds of War*. New York: Basic Books, Inc., 1984.

Holmes, Arthur F., ed. *War and Christian Ethics*. Grand Rapids: Baker Book House, 1975.

Holmes, R. *Acts of War: The Behavior of Men in Battle*. New York: The Free Press, 1986.

Kilpatrick, M.A. "Coping With Survival." *Aircraft Disasters and Emergency: Guidelines for Psycho-Emotional Recovery*, 1981. 431 N. Brand Boulevard, Suite 313, Glendale, California 91302.

McCaughey, B.G. "U.S. Navy Special Psychiatric Rapid Intervention Team (SPRINT)." *Military Medicine* 152, 3(1987):133–135.

Milgram, Norman. *Stress and Coping in Time of War*. New York: Brunner/Mazel Publishers, 1986.

Mitchell, J.T. "When Disaster Strikes . . . the Critical Incidents Stress Debriefing Process." *Journal of Emergency Medical Services* 8(January 1983):36–39.

Mitchell, J.T., and Resnik, H.L.P. *Emergency Response to Crisis*. Baltimore: Robert J. Brady Company, 1981.

National Institute of Mental Health. *Training Manual for Human Service Workers in Major Disasters*. Washington, DC: U.S. Government Printing Office, 1978.

Nouwen, Henri J. *The Wounded Healer*. Garden City, New York: Image Books, 1979.

Price, V.R. "Grief Work and Dirty Work: The Aftermath of an Air Crash." *Omega* 5,4(1974):281–286.

Ramsey, Paul. *War and the Christian Conscience*. Durham, North Carolina: Duke University Press, 1961.

Segal, Julius. *Winning Life's Toughest Battles*. New York: McGraw-Hill Book Company, 1986.

Taylor, A.J.W., and Frazer, A.G. "The Stress of Post-disaster Body Handling and Victim Identification Work." *Journal of Human Stress*, December 1982, 4–12.